CAPTAIN
JAMES COOK:
Genius Afloat

CAPTAIN JAMES COOK:

Genius Afloat

by
Daniel J. Carrison,
Captain, U.S.N. (Ret.)

Franklin Watts, Inc.
575 Lexington Avenue
New York, N.Y. 10022

To Aurela, on our Twenty-fifth Anniversary

Jacket photo courtesy of
The Bettmann Archive, Inc.

CONTENTS

PREFACE

Captain James Cook, a self-made, self-taught practical genius, was the greatest explorer of his age. His pioneering discoveries and contributions to knowledge place him on a level with Columbus, Ferdinand Magellan, Marco Polo, and David Livingstone.

English biographers assert that Americans hold Cook in lower estimation than they should. There is some truth in this criticism, for Captain Cook's memory was smeared by jealous missionaries in Hawaii during the early part of the nineteenth century.

Cook was a great sailor and a man of character. He deserves as much admiration and respect today as he commanded nearly two hundred years ago, when Benjamin Franklin guaranteed him safe passage home during the American Revolution.

Daniel J. Carrison,
Captain, U.S.N. (Ret.)

PART I

Preparation

CHAPTER ONE

YEARS OF APPRENTICESHIP

THE voyages of Captain James Cook, who has been called the greatest sailor in history, changed the face of the world. This quiet, determined English explorer reached the height of his fame at the time of the American Revolution. His explorations were considered so important to furthering the world's knowledge that in 1776, during the American Revolution, Benjamin Franklin sent letters to all American men-of-war, advising them to let Cook pass unharmed.

Captain Cook was, said Franklin, on a voyage "to discover new countries in unknown seas" and the enterprise promised "to expand the progress of all sciences useful to the human race." He went on: "I strongly desire that those of you who meet Captain Cook's ship, which is now awaited in European waters, should not regard him as an enemy. . . ."

France and Spain, traditional foes of Great Britain, who were also at war with that island kingdom, followed Franklin's inspiration and issued orders to their fleets not to interfere with Captain Cook.

During the eighteenth century, Great Britain was

more interested in exploration than she had been at any other time. The scientific era had just begun, and the great powers of Europe were in a life-and-death struggle for control of world commerce. Famous voyages had brought riches and power to countries that had had the foresight to promote exploration. Yet many of these ventures had failed, either through unfortunate circumstances or the inadequacies of the expedition's commander. But in James Cook, Great Britain found a genius who had all of the qualities necessary to command, explore unknown waters, and make the clearest and most accurate charts in the history of exploration.

There had been good navigators before Cook, but men such as Quiros and Dampier could not command and were continually threatened with mutiny. Other famous sailors, like Magellan, Tasman, and Anson, were defeated or hampered by scurvy. Men like Drake and Hawkins were essentially pirates, whose primary interest lay in booty.

Thus it fell to Cook, who was at once a seaman, a navigator, a cartographer, an explorer, a scientist, an astronomer, and a leader, to sail and chart the Pacific Ocean as had never been done before. The sheer volume of his work was monumental, and its accuracy was amazing. For more than one hundred years after his death in 1779, sailors around the world were using his charts and sailing directions essentially unchanged. Perhaps the greatest of the French explorers, Captain La Perouse, spoke for all seamen when he said of Cook's achievements, ". . . Mr. Cook has done so much that he has left me nothing to do but to admire his work."

One of the most miraculous of James Cook's accomplishments was his rise from a humble beginning, for in eighteenth century England, it was difficult to break the class barrier. Born the son of a day laborer in the village of Marton, Yorkshire, on October 27, 1728, James Cook spent his early years in a series of successful attempts to improve his lot.

He was a bright youngster who attracted the attention of his elders. The first evidence of this is recorded by a generous act of his father's employer, Thomas Scottowe, who sent young James to school. There the boy showed an eagerness to learn and a flair for figures. Soon he had absorbed all that the small village school could teach him, and with the restlessness of youth, James set out to further improve his station.

At the age of 17 he was apprenticed to William Sanderson, who owned a general store in Staithes, a small fishing village on the Yorkshire coast. Fascinated by the water, young Cook worked hard for a year and a half, then persuaded his employer to release him so that he could go to sea. It is remarkable that at this time, and on subsequent occasions when Cook left a position in his upward struggle, his superiors were willing to help him. Mr. Sanderson gave him his blessing, and better still, he gave him a letter of introduction to John Walker, a shipowner in the nearby port of Whitby.

At last James Cook was a sailor. He signed the articles of apprenticeship with Mr. Walker for a period of three years. John Walker and his sons were coastal coal traders, who operated their seaworthy collier *Freelove* in the North Sea and the Baltic. Cook could not have picked a better place to learn his trade. The North Sea, with its bitter winds, strong currents, fog, and rough water, was a great proving ground. Only a skillful seaman could survive in such waters, let alone operate his ship at a profit.

The Walkers prospered, threading the narrow channels in their sturdy little boat with consummate skill. They soon learned that their gawky, six-foot apprentice was exceptional. He was quick-witted, he remembered things, he mastered figures easily, and he was eager to learn. During the long winter rest between voyages, James studied Mr. Walker's books on navigation.

After three years, Cook moved to other shipping lines, signing on as an able seaman. He continued to cruise in the North Sea and the Baltic, acquiring more experience and ability with each passing year. When he was twenty-four he returned to the Walkers and became mate of the collier *Friendship*. This was a meteoric rise for a landsman—from apprentice to the responsible position of mate in only six years. Mr. Walker's faith in James was vindicated. After three successful years as mate, James Cook had become such a competent merchant seaman that Mr. Walker decided to appoint him captain of one of his ships.

A lesser man, or at least one who did not have an irresistible urge for far horizons, would have accepted the honor eagerly. This was the ultimate symbol of success in the maritime world—to be master of a merchant ship. After only eight years James Cook had arrived; his future and his financial security as a mariner were assured. But, instead of remaining with the Walkers and accepting the position of master, he took the unpredictable alternative of enlisting in the Royal Navy as an able-bodied seaman. He had outgrown the North Sea and was now willing to toss away his hard-earned rank in order to see more of the world.

Once again Cook's rise was amazing. Among the untrained landlubbers who were pressed into service as England began the Seven Years' War, James Cook stood out like a beacon. In a little over a month he was made master's mate of HMS *Eagle*. Shortly afterward the *Eagle* received a new captain. He was Hugh Palliser, who, at the age of 23, had already shown the promise which later was to see him lord of the Admiralty, baronet, and admiral.

A bond soon sprang up between these two able young men. Though they were miles apart with respect to birth and upbringing, they had a mutual admiration for each other's seamanship. Cook's reliability and competence so impressed Palliser that scarcely two months had elapsed before he promoted the tall Yorkshireman to boatswain.

The *Eagle* joined other ships of the fleet in blockading the coasts of France. During this long watch offshore, Cook had his first acquaintance with the sailor's nemesis on long voyages—scurvy. In 1756, Captain Palliser wrote one of his superiors that in one month alone he had buried twenty-two of the crew and had landed one hundred and thirty wasted men for the hospital—all victims of scurvy. Cook's inquisitive mind noted that there had been less scurvy in his experience with the merchant marine, whose ships were more frequently in and out of port. He also noticed that the disease singled out men in inverse order of rank. The forecastle gang, who subsisted primarily on a monotonous diet of salt meat and biscuits, were much more susceptible to sickness than were the officers, who were able to set a good table.

In those days, rather than take corrective action, the Admiralty simply accepted the ravages of scurvy as a fact of naval life. It was one of their "planning factors" on long voyages. Assuming that there would be large losses, they deliberately overstaffed their ships to offset casualties. Seamen were expendable. It was only necessary to plan sufficiently well to ensure the safety of the ship; after that, it was up to the press gangs to find the required number of men. Scurvy was a deficiency disease which literally rotted bodies away. Cook's brush with it on the *Eagle* made an indelible impression on him; not only was it inhuman to accept scurvy as inevitable but it was also inefficient. In later years, Captain Cook was to take great pride in showing the world how simply the disease could be conquered.

From his first day in the navy, young Cook kept a log. How he found time to do this in the cold, dark, cramped living spaces aboard ship after ship is hard to say. Fortunately, this habit stayed with him throughout his life, and because of it the world has a thorough insight into this great man's inner thoughts and character. During his early years, Cook's first entries were limited to a seaman's observations; he would note currents, winds, soundings, nature of the bottom, and the cargo received and discharged, and he would embellish the margins with explanatory sketches. As he developed mentally and his interests expanded, his journal entries broadened to include lucid descriptions of the strange lands he visited and peoples he met.

With service in the English Channel and the Bay of Biscay now behind him, Cook was ready for blue water. He asked for a new assignment, and at the same time requested a king's commission. Once again his superior supported him. Captain Hugh Palliser recognized Cook's great ability, so he recommended him highly. Cook's old friend and employer, John Walker, also joined in support. In earlier years this might have sufficed, but the Admiralty had just adopted a new rule for eligibility; a man had to serve for six years in the navy before he could be commissioned. James Cook had served only two years. Accordingly he was given the next best thing: He was appointed a warrant master and was assigned to the *Pembroke*, a sixty-four-gun ship of the line. Here Cook's meteoric rise ended. Ten long years were to pass before he was able to realize his ambition of becoming a commissioned officer.

The duties of a master in those days were demanding. He had to supervise the ship's routine, and more important, he was required to act as sailing master, navigator, and pilot. The *Pembroke*'s first voyage was a challenge for the new master. The ship left England and crossed the Atlantic against unfavorable winds, taking eleven weeks instead of the customary three. The *Pembroke* was scheduled to take part in the assault on Louisburg at Cape Breton Island, which had to be destroyed before a force under General Wolfe could mount an attack on Quebec. However, the ship's crew was so riddled with scurvy that they had to put into Halifax for a short rest and cure. The crew recovered quickly, and the *Pembroke* rejoined the fleet at Louisburg in time for the amphibious attack that brought about the fort's surrender.

The fleet wintered over in Halifax and moved out again in the spring for an all-out assault on Quebec. General Wolfe, remembering how a British expedition had foundered in the St. Lawrence River fifty years before, demanded that the approaches to Quebec be surveyed and charted. The task fell to Cook and other shipmasters. In a short while Cook's mastery of figures and his tireless, meticulous charting were recognized throughout the squadron. General Wolfe himself, as well as senior naval officers, consulted with him and sought his advice. He became unofficially known as "master surveyor of the fleet."

After the fall of Quebec in 1759, Cook was transferred to the *Northumberland* to become master of the flagship. In this capacity he continued to survey rivers and coasts as opportunities presented themselves. Many of the ships returned to England that summer, but the *Northumberland* remained behind to winter over in Halifax. During this period of inactivity, James Cook spent most of his time in his small cabin studying geometry and astronomy. He had no tutor—just a few textbooks and his own inquisitive mind.

Another summer and another winter passed. The fleet traversed the St. Lawrence again and coasted the difficult waters around Newfoundland. Cook continued his indefatigable surveying, making chart after chart, checking them carefully, and then stowing them away. Captain Colville of the *Northumberland* sent many of them back to England for publication, and showed his appreciation by the following official action. He directed the purser "to pay the Master of the *Northumberland* fifty pounds in consideration of his indefatigable industry in making himself master of the pilotage of the River St. Lawrence."

After an absence of four long years, Cook returned to England on the *Northumberland*. He was thirty-four years old and still a bachelor. It is characteristic of the man that his log, which was replete with nautical facts, contained no mention of his first romance. Less than a month after his return, he married Elizabeth Batts, the daughter of a London shopkeeper who was many "stations" above the son of a day laborer, but the equal of a warrant master of His Majesty's Navy. It was a fine, unspectacular marriage which brought forth six children before Cook's untimely death. Elizabeth, who was twenty-one when she married, lived to survive her husband and all of her children as well; she died at the remarkable age of ninety-three.

The newlyweds settled in a house on Mile End Road on the outskirts of London. It was a pleasant anchorage which beckoned James Cook like a lodestone when he returned from each voyage. And voyage he did. Within four months after his wedding, he was on his way back to Newfoundland as "Mr. J. Cook, Engineer." His pay was an unusual ten shillings a day in return for completing a survey of the coasts of Newfoundland.

In his second year on the Newfoundland survey, Cook's old captain and admirer, now Sir Hugh Palliser, became governor of Newfoundland. Presumably at Palliser's urging, the Admiralty gave Cook a ship of his own for finishing out the survey. It was the small schooner *Grenville*, which required a crew of only ten men. It was small enough to work close to shore without danger, but it was a challenge for even a seaman of Cook's ability to sail it across the North Atlantic.

However, for four years Cook and his men would cross the Atlantic in the spring and then return to England for the winter. These were pleasant years for Cook. During the cold winter months he lived at home and worked on his charts at a special desk in the Admiralty. Elizabeth bore him children with regularity, and the wandering sailor felt the creeping clutches of domesticity.

At first Cook's success as a surveyor overshadowed his ability as a seaman. However, after a while, senior officers in the Admiralty noticed a peculiarity of the *Grenville*. She came and went with clocklike precision. She remained at sea for long periods of time but her crew remained healthy. In all of his crossings in the North Atlantic aboard this pitifully small boat, James Cook did not lose a man. His men signed on to stay with him year after year, which was remarkable at a time when many men preferred prison to going to sea.

During the cruise of 1766, Cook computed the time of an eclipse of the sun and observed it on a small island off Newfoundland. He presented his report to the Royal Society in London, where it was received with raised eyebrows. Who was this Cook? Where had he studied? How could a self-taught sailor from the farm fields of Yorkshire make such an accurate observation? To that great scientific body's credit, the Society accepted his precise report and published it, noting that it was the product of surveyor J. Cook, who was "a good mathematician and very expert in his business."

Home for the winter of 1767–68, Cook settled down to work on his charts at the Admiralty. While he labored at his desk, events of great personal importance to him were gathering momentum. Two separate but related quests, each calling for a man of Cook's abilities, had caught England's fancy. First, there was an expected transit of Venus, which the Royal Society wished to observe. Second, the Admiralty was required to furnish a ship and crew to take the observation party to a suitable site.

The transit of Venus aroused the interest of the scientific community because it offered a chance for a more accurate determination of the earth's distance from the sun—something that was basic to certain calculations necessary for improved navigation. The transit had been predicted years before by the Royal Astronomer Edmund Halley, who pointed out that after the transit in 1769, another would not occur for one hundred years. The Society established a committee to determine the best locations for a thorough observation. The committee decided upon two sites in the northern hemisphere and a site in the southern hemisphere near the Tropic of Capricorn, about halfway across the Pacific. The locations at the North Cape of Norway and at Hudson Bay in Canada did not present any great problem. But the site in the Pacific was halfway around the world, and there were innumerable problems in transporting an observation party there.

The Royal Society advised King George that several other countries were readying expeditions, and strongly recommended that England participate for her own interests as well as in the interest of science. In particular they sought the Crown's support for a ship. Time was pressing, because it would take roughly a year's lead time to equip a ship and have it on station in time for the transit. King George acquiesced and granted funds in the amount of £4,000 to subsidize the project. He ordered the Admiralty to furnish a suitable ship.

The Society was pleased and selected Alexander Dalrymple, a Society member with scientific qualifications and some experience at exploration, to be chief observer. Dalrymple was a hot-tempered Scot who had a great opinion of himself. He agreed to go, but only on the condition that he would be in command. The Admiralty would have none of it. Too often in their navy's history they had come to grief with this sort of arrangement. There were too many dangers, and experience had shown them that scientific experts had been poor commanders. Astronomer Halley was a good example—his crew had mutinied when he captained a navy ship during an expedition. The Admiralty stubbornly insisted that a naval officer had to command, and pointed out that they could not appoint Dalrymple an officer because of the rule that a man had to serve in the navy for six years before he was eligible for a commission. In all fairness to the Admiralty, this was a good rule, and it was an excellent hedge to use when some prominent man would try to use influence in order to obtain a commission. Moreover, the Admiralty secretly planned to send the ship on a voyage of discovery in the Pacific after the transit observation had been completed. It was not until the year 1928 that these exact orders were discovered in old records of the British navy, and it is evident from them that the Admiralty had in mind a voyage of two or more years. Thus it was little wonder they wanted an experienced commander and expert seaman to see it through.

Some of James Cook's "friends in high places" (as he later referred to them) submitted his name, and he was quickly accepted. Cook was a proven surveyor and an excellent seaman, and he was known by the Society. The navy, at long last, and well after the required minimum of six years' service, made James Cook a lieutenant, and put him in charge of the venture. He was now forty years old, already an "old man" in the youthful British navy, when he finally realized his ambition of becoming a commissioned naval officer.

CHAPTER TWO

LURE OF THE PACIFIC

AT the time Captain Cook lived, the world knew enough about the Pacific Ocean to be greatly intrigued by it. European scholars first heard of this great, challenging body of water from the writings of Marco Polo, who traveled extensively over central and southern Asia in the thirteenth century. Near the close of the fifteenth century, when Columbus' "voyage to Cathay" ended with the discovery of a new continent, the world realized that between the broad boundaries of America on the East and China on the West, there lay a great ocean.

From 1497 to 1499 the explorer Vasco da Gama rounded the southern tip of Africa off the Cape of Good Hope and pioneered the sailing route to India. Shortly afterward, in 1513, Balboa crossed the Isthmus of Panama and became the first European to see the Pacific. He promptly claimed it in the name of the King of Spain and called it Mar del Zur—the South Sea. It was left to Ferdinand Magellan, seven years later, to pass through the straits at the southern end of South America and to give the ocean a name that has endured ever since—Pacific. Thus the outlines of the Pacific gradually emerged and the world was eager to learn what lay between its extremities.

In the nearly two and a half centuries that elapsed before Captain Cook's first voyage, some of these details came to light. Magellan's epic voyage from 1519 to 1521 proved that the earth could be circumnavigated. It also revealed the thin margin of safety for a wind-driven ship traversing this great expanse of water. The hardships of Magellan's men, who would pay a ducat for a rat and were driven to eating their belts and shoe leather, convinced other seamen that Vasco da Gama's route to the Orient was by far the easier and safer way.

The exploration of the Pacific had attracted a number of Spanish, Portuguese, Dutch, and English sailors. The Portuguese led the way in the sixteenth century, seizing control of the best West Indian ports. They were soon hard pressed by the Dutch, who established thriving settlements at Java and other suitable ports in the East Indies. With the exception of interests in the Philippines, which they owed to Magellan, the Spanish were satisfied to concentrate on the lucrative trade in precious metals around the west coasts of America.

In the ensuing years, most of the western voyagers across the Pacific followed the trail blazed by Magellan, which was understandable, since their ships relied on fair winds to avoid disaster. Even with strong southeast trades helping them, the specter of hunger and thirst hovered just over the horizon. Each succeeding voyage had these pioneers discovering small islands along the track where tired ships and men could pause and replenish provisions and fresh water. Because of the difficulties, the lower half of the Pacific, south of Magellan's route, remained a great unknown expanse of water until Cook came on the scene.

These early sailors would find and report islands that

would afterward remain hidden for years. The Solomons, for example, were not rediscovered for two hundred years simply because the original reported position was so inaccurate. For several centuries navigators and astronomers had been able to find latitude with reasonable accuracy, but longitude was another story. Seventeenth century astronomer Gellibrand, describing Captain Thomas James's voyage in 1631, noted that "for exact settings of latitude we have many and absolute helps . . . but the longitude of a meridian is that which hath and still wearieth the greatest masters of geography."

Nevertheless, as each little pearl of information about the Pacific was found, geographers would string a necklace of fact and fancy to explain and describe the Pacific. According to the best thought at the time, there was a vast hidden continent in the South Pacific that lay somewhere between the Cape of Good Hope and the Strait of Magellan. One theory, believed by many, was that the earth needed a landmass in that part of the globe for balance; symmetry demanded it. The geographers called this land Terra Australis Incognita.

In the latter part of the sixteenth century, Dutch ships touched the barren western and northwestern coasts of Australia. Disappointed in finding such a wasteland, they did not bother to explore inland, but just gave it the name of New Holland, assuming it was an extension of New Guinea. A Dutch sailor named Abel Tasman was the first to prove that this land did not extend to the South Pole. Under the sponsorship of energetic Governor Van Dieman, Tasman sailed west from Mauritius in latitudes generally above 40 degrees south and passed between "New Holland" and the Antarctic. He touched at the island now called Tasmania, and then proceeded north to discover New Zealand, which he called "Staten Island." The ferocious Maoris discouraged a landing, so Tasman did not exploit his discovery. He pushed on to Batavia, and reported that he had found the northwestern tip of the unknown southern continent.

Until Captain Cook proved that this continent did not exist except as a frozen waste in the Antarctic, it remained an obsession of seafaring countries. In the early eighteenth century, daring circumnavigators like Anson, Byron, Bougainville, and Wallis made a series of discoveries in the main island chains of the Pacific, but none touched the east coast of Australia. Each new discovery prompted geographers to go a little further in their development of theories. Alexander Dalrymple stated positively that Terra Australis Incognita had a population of fifty million. He and his colleagues described this strange land and its wealth so well that the tradesmen of Europe eagerly pressed their governments for more expeditions to discover it; for the nation that made first contact and claimed this continent could become fabulously wealthy. A wave of eagerness in England was borne on the fear that either France or Spain would find Terra Australis first.

The time was ripe for great voyages of exploration. Developments in navigation during the eighteenth century produced the quadrant and the chronometer, which enabled a navigator to fix his position with far greater accuracy than before. Gradually, seamen learned about the pattern of winds and currents around the world, and established routes that would put these elements to work for them.

The great oceans—the North Atlantic and South Atlantic, North Pacific and South Pacific, and the Indian Ocean—had a system of winds that was fairly standard. Above the equator they moved in a clockwise direction, while south of the equator they were counterclockwise. The systems had identifiable variations. They were seasonal, moving either north or south with the sun; and they were influenced by large landmasses. Ocean currents, such as the Gulf Stream, were recognized and put to use by combining them with the prevailing winds to produce the most efficient sailing routes. Often the best route for a sailing ship was not the shortest distance, but the one which had favorable winds.

For example, the standard route from Europe to the Dutch East Indies led across the Atlantic to the coast of Brazil, where ships could pick up the southeast trades. They would then glide to the Cape of Good Hope and pick up westerlies on a wild run to the longitude of Java, where they would swing north into the trades and on to their destination. This practice did not require very accurate navigation. Captains would use rules of thumb, instinct, or just blind luck. Thus they would sail "south til' the butter melts, then east," and hope they would make a landfall from which they could take an accurate departure.

The chronometer, a precision watch which was carefully mounted on gimbals and stored in a felt-lined box, gave navigators the correct time at Greenwich. This they compared to local time, determined by celestial observation, in order to compute longitude. Prior to the eighteenth century, navigators dead-reckoned longitude or obtained it by the lunar method. This was laborious and was accurate only in the hands of the most skilled navigators. The observer had to measure the angle between the sun or a star and the moon, while his assistants observed the altitude of the two bodies. When the chronometer was introduced aboard ships, it made the problem much easier to solve, and was considered so necessary to navigation that, in 1765, a prize of £10,000 was paid to John Harrison of England for making a chronometer that would keep accurate time at sea.

Captain Cook computed longitude by the lunar method during his first voyage. However, during his second and third voyages he took along a chronometer and thereafter became one of its staunchest advocates.

As the time came for Cook's voyage, there was great excitement in England. There was a sense of anticipation, and an awakening to the new vistas that scientific advance had made possible. Cook knew of only one insoluble problem that remained. There still was no cure for scurvy.

CHAPTER THREE

SHIP AND CREW

WHEN King George approved the Royal Society's request for an expedition to the Pacific, he ordered the Admiralty to provide a suitable ship forthwith. Historians have tried to connect Cook with the navy's choice of the bark *Endeavor*, but records to prove this association are not available. It is known, however, that the Admiralty picked the vessel before they appointed her captain. Nevertheless, there seems to be a coincidence between Cook's early merchant experience on Whitby-built colliers and the navy's selection of a Whitby collier for this important voyage. On March 29, 1768, the navy board purchased the *Earl of Pembroke* for a little over £2,300, and entered her on the navy register as the bark *Endeavor* to distinguish her from another ship of the same original name.

The newly christened *Endeavor* was moved to the Deptford yards on the Thames River for alterations. These were necessary to change her from a collier to a navy ship fitted out for an extended voyage. The collier was admirably suited for the task, being a three-masted square rigger of 368-ton displacement. By comparison to modern ships, the *Endeavor* was extremely small, 106 feet long overall, with a beam of 29 feet, 3 inches, but she was quite safe and a good sailer. In seamen's terms, the ship was "cat built," which meant that she had wide bows and a thick, deep waist that tapered near the stern. Unlike swifter men-of-war and sleek merchant ships that could knife through the water, the *Endeavor* sailed more like a barrel, but, with her rounded bottom, she had one essential advantage—she could be beached in shallow water for repairs without tumbling over.

After he had completed his famous first voyage, Captain Cook described the *Endeavor's* advantages as follows:

A ship of this kind must not be of a great draught of water, yet of a sufficient burden and capacity to carry a proper quantity of provisions and necessaries for her compliment of men, and for the term requisite to perform the voyage. She must also be of a construction that will bear to take the ground, and of a size which, in case of necessity, may be safely and conveniently laid on shore to repair any accidental damage or defect.

He went on to say,

These properties are not to be found in ships of war of forty guns, nor in frigates, nor in East India Company's ships, nor in large three-decked West India ships, nor indeed in any other but North-Country ships such as are built for the coal trade, which are peculiarly adapted for this purpose.

Once committed to the task, the Admiralty was eager to outfit the ship as well as possible. Shipwrights made alterations below decks to accommodate her crew and built spaces to house a large store of provisions and scientific instruments. The *Endeavor's* bottom did not have copper sheathing, which was the newest method for protecting wooden hulls from tropical sea worms, but she was given a wood sheathing, or skin, of thinner boards outside her main planking. It is believed that Cook objected to copper on the grounds that it would be too great a problem for repair on distant shores. Because of sea worms, as well as the usual wear and tear from routine usage, wooden ships of those days were given a life expectancy of about ten years. In 1768 the *Endeavor* was four years old, really her best age—she had been shaken down and seasoned, but was still youthful.

The Royal Society also had a hand in the preparations. First they put aboard telescopes and other instruments to be used in observing the transit of Venus. Next, they obtained permission to expand the scope of the expedition to include a party of botanists, who would be able to bring back useful information concerning the strange lands. To head this party they chose a very unusual young man, Joseph Banks, a gentleman of large fortune and a member of the Society. He was a high-spirited, hardy, impetuous man who had already shown brilliance as a botanist in an expedition to Newfoundland.

Joseph Banks spent an estimated £10,000 of his own fortune on the voyage. He brought with him, and paid the salaries of, an associate botanist, Dr. Daniel Solander, and a retinue of assistants, artists, and servants. He stored aboard the *Endeavor* a variety of jars, lenses, preservatives for specimens, salts, waxes (for keeping seeds), and special traps for catching insects. Accustomed to pleasant living, he equipped his cabin with little luxuries, and from all accounts, seemed to survive the entire voyage in fine spirits. He and James Cook became firm friends, and each had respect for the other. It is interesting to note in Cook's journal how his eager mind grasped the essentials of this new field, and how his interests broadened under the influence of this learned man in the ship's company.

Dr. Solander was a Swedish botanist who had studied under the famous Linnaeus and had emigrated to England nine years before the expedition was formed. He was recognized in England as an authority on natural history and an excellent librarian, and was considered to be one of the ablest botanists of the time. He spoke excellent English, was quite sophisticated, and made a good companion for the impetuous Banks. Unfortunately his pursuit of pleasure interfered with his work in later years. When he died of a stroke about eleven years after the great voyage, he had not completed and published the volumes that he had maintained on the *Endeavor*.

Alexander Buchan and Sydney Parkinson were the artists; the former specializing in landscapes, the latter an expert in biological and botanical sketching. Poor Buchan proved to be an epileptic who should never have sailed on an arduous voyage, and he died shortly after the ship reached Tahiti.

The Royal Society determined that the expedition needed two observers to take accurate measurements during the transit of Venus. Originally they had expected Alexander Dalrymple to be the chief observer, but when he withdrew in a pique, they had to search for a substitute. Charles Green, assistant to the Royal Astronomer, had already been nominated as one of the observers. The logical choice for the second was none other than Cook himself. He had shown ability in his observation of the eclipse of 1766, and he had impressed Society members favorably during a personal interview. So the authorities of that institution picked this self-taught genius for one of the most important astronomical tasks of the times. They agreed to pay Cook 100 guineas as the second observer, and added an additional allowance of £120 a year for Green and Cook to use in maintaining their mess. Cook felt very fortunate indeed, for in addition to these sums his rate of pay as a lieutenant in the navy was 5 shillings a day.

The problem of finding a crew for the long voyage normally would have been a difficult one, but Cook's reputation on the waterfront was a great asset. Five of the men who had sailed with him on the *Grenville* signed on. One of the officers and three seamen who had sailed with Wallis when he discovered Tahiti also joined. While Cook did have a hand in picking several key men, like the gunner, the boatswain, and the armorer, he was unable to exercise much influence in the selection of a cook. The first one assigned was a cripple, and the incensed Cook wrote the Admiralty that he was a "lame, infirm man, incapable of doing his duty without assistance of others." The second cook that the navy gave him had only one hand. Though Cook objected to him also, he could not prevail again. Curiously enough, the one-handed cook, John Thompson, proved to be one of the best in the navy. In all of the journals kept on the *Endeavor*, there were no derogatory remarks about the cook. This would be unusual even today, when ships' cooks have modern galleys and every conceivable laborsaving device.

As navigator's stores Cook carried a complete library of available charts and books of the Pacific. The Admiralty gave him the log of Captain Wallis, discoverer of Tahiti, who had returned from his circumnavigation of the globe just a few months earlier (March, 1768). Since Wallis was a respected professional who had documented the position of Tahiti accurately, both the Society and the Admiralty agreed to that island as the location for the observation of the Venus transit. Captain Cook had no qualms about locating Tahiti or getting there in time, so there was mutual accord with the decision.

At forty years of age, James Cook was an impressive figure. Tall, reserved, and dignified, he stood erect and was not shy about his height of six feet, which was more unusual in the eighteenth century than it is today. His journals reveal his common sense and depth of feeling, and display almost immediately the qualities that marked him as one of nature's gentlemen. Except for his portrait and impressions left by his contemporaries, there is very little of his own records that describe the man and his personality. His men thought that he was an unusually gentle disciplinarian, and marveled at the detail with which he looked out for their well-being and the cleanliness of their quarters. They swore that he could smell land, and mentioned the many times that he had appeared on deck in the dead of night and ordered a course change. Daylight would inevitably show that the ship had been heading into an unknown danger.

A contemporary who sailed with him on the third voyage, Lieutenant James King, had this to say about his indifference to creature comforts: "Temperance in him was scarcely a virtue; so great was the indifference with which he submitted to every kind of self-denial."

Cook never asked his men to do anything that he would not do himself. For example, when he decided that fresh onions would help the men in their fight against scurvy, he purchased a huge store of them in Madeira and prescribed about thirty pounds per man. Manfully he ate his share.

James Cook was an austere man. His wife Elizabeth always referred to him as "Mr. Cook." His men on his first command, and on all of his subsequent commands, swore by him. For although he was austere and business-like, he had an easy way with men, without being familiar. When he once became seriously ill, the crew could hardly believe that their quiet, stern leader could succumb to any illness. To a man, they tiptoed about the decks, anxiously asking his attendants for signs of improvement. When he finally recovered (with the help of meat broth, for which the men sacrificed the ship's pet dog) they all breathed a sigh of relief.

Cook was the ideal leader for a long, dangerous voyage. Physically he was strong; generally he could endure anything and eat anything. Moreover, he was completely unafraid. His strength of character, competence, and close attention to detail endured through the years, and were the primary reasons why his expeditions survived innumerable dangers and hardships. He took his ships and men into unknown waters and delighted in sailing close to dangerous shores in order to identify them. Other seamen would take a more prudent course and give many of Cook's beaches a wide berth. Cook was able to take his crews well beyond previous limits of endurance without harm, simply because of his forethought, his abiding interest in their well-being, and their respect and trust in him.

It was on Friday, May 27, 1768, when James Cook

finally realized his life's ambition. The first entry in his journal hardly reflects the pride and sense of satisfaction that he must have felt that day:

Moderate and fair weather, at 11am hoisted the pendant and took charge of the Ship agreeable to my commission of the 25th Instant, she lying in the Bason in Deptford Yard.

(A self-taught man, Cook was an exceedingly accurate mathematician, but he never quite mastered spelling.)

For almost two months the *Endeavor* took on stores and filled out her crew. On July 21, the ship got under sail for Plymouth. Bad weather held up her departure, but Cook kept busy taking on fresh beef, bread, beer, rum, and water. Shipwrights put finishing touches on the "gentlemen's cabins," and on August 25 Captain Cook "loosed the topsails as a signal for sailing." This brought Joseph Banks and his assistants aboard. At 2:00 P.M. on the twenty-sixth all was in readiness, and the *Endeavor* took departure from her home shores. Officials in the Admiralty took justifiable satisfaction in her condition, remarking that never before had a ship sailed so well fitted out for her mission. Cook's log entry for the day bears this out:

At 2pm got under sail and put to sea having on board 94 persons including Officers, Seamen, Gentlemen and their servants, near 18 months of provisions, 10 Carriage guns, 12 Swivels with a good store of ammunition and stores of all kinds.

PART II

The First Voyage

CHAPTER FOUR

SHAKEDOWN CRUISE

THE first voyage of a new navy ship is usually called a shakedown cruise. Both ship and crew need an early period of breaking in, of becoming familiar with each other's habits and idiosyncrasies, before they make a good team. This age-old practice is still followed today; even nuclear-powered ships of the most modern design go on a shakedown cruise before reporting to the operating fleet for more demanding assignments.

The *Endeavor*'s shakedown cruise to Tahiti was slow and uneventful. By the time she had fought her way past Cape Horn, the crew knew the ship and how she behaved under many variations of wind and sea. They had learned to live in harmony in their cramped quarters, and were able to interpret every creak of the mast and rigging. Even the "gentlemen" and their servants blended in with the routine. And everyone, from the learned scientists down to the lowest seaman, knew that the captain of the *Endeavor* was a master of his trade.

The weather around the Bay of Biscay was rough, causing Cook to note in his journal that "very hard gales" had caused the loss of a small boat and drowned between three and four dozen poultry, "which was worst of all." After a week of fairly dirty weather and slow progress, the *Endeavor* caught a favorable breeze toward Madeira, the first port of call and a stop specifically ordered in the Admiralty's instructions. Neither water nor beer would keep well on long voyages, so ships generally stopped at Madeira for wine before setting out across the Atlantic.

Actually, Captain Cook's instructions were remarkably detailed and concise. The Admiralty commissioners first ordered him to pay his crew two months' wages in advance at Plymouth, then to take on the scientific observers, then to put to sea and stop at Madeira for wine. From there he was told to proceed around Cape Horn to Port Royal in King George's Island (Tahiti). He had permission to touch the coast of Brazil and Falkland Isles as necessary to procure water and "refreshments for the Bark's Company." With the thoroughness of experienced seamen, the commissioners included the best sailing instructions available, the deadline of the transit (June 3, 1769), and the geographical limits for the southern observation in the unlikely event that Cook could not reach Tahiti and had to find an alternate location.

The unclassified instructions referred to a separate set of secret sealed instructions which were to be opened after the observation of the transit had been completed. For reasons that still remain a mystery, these secret instructions were lost to historians until 1928, when they were unearthed in old files of the British navy. Whether or not Captain Cook waited approximately a year before opening the sealed packet is unknown, but most men would have taken a look long before then. These instructions reflect accurately the background, the intense feeling, and air of urgency that prevailed at the time:

SECRET   By the Commissioners for executing the office of Lord High Admiral of Great Britain, Etc.

Additional instructions for Lt. James Cook, Appointed to Command His Majesty's Bark the Endeavor.

Whereas the making of Discoveries of Countries hitherto unknown, and the Attaining a knowledge of distant parts which though formerly discovered have yet been but imperfectly explored, will redound greatly to the Honor of this Nation as a Maritime Power, as well as to the Dignity of the Crown of Great Britain, and may tend greatly to the advancement of the Trade and Navigation thereof; and Whereas there is reason to imagine that a Continent or Land of great extent, may be found to the Southward of the Tract lately made by Captain Wallis in His Majesty's Ship the Dolphin (of which you will herewith receive a copy) or of the Tract of any former Navigators in Pursuits of the like kind; You are therefore in Pursuance of His Majesty's Pleasure hereby required and directed to put to Sea with the Bark you Command so soon as the Observation of the Transit of Venus shall be finished and observe the following instructions . . .

Captain Cook must have read the remainder of the packet with great relish. He was instructed to proceed southward from Tahiti in search of this new land until he reached latitude of 40 degrees, "unless you sooner fall in with it." If he failed to discover it on that run, he was to proceed westward between the 40th and 35th parallels of south latitude until he discovered it or fell in "with the eastern side of the land discovered by Tasman and now called New Zealand." If he discovered the continent, his first responsibility was to explore the coast with diligence, surveying and making charts. Next he was to observe the nature of the soil, its products, animal life, and valuable stones or minerals, and bring home such seeds of trees, fruits, and grains that he could collect. Should he fail to find the continent entirely, and only reach New Zealand, he was to explore it in a similar fashion insofar as the health of his men and the condition of his ship would permit. Afterward he was to return to England around either the Cape of Good Hope or Cape Horn, as he deemed best. Whatever lands or islands he discovered were to be claimed for England.

It might be difficult for a reader in the mid-twentieth century to comprehend the challenge that lay in Captain Cook's second set of instructions. Two hundred years ago one of the greatest fears of mankind was the fear of the unknown. The Admiralty commissioners had ordered Cook to take his bark into uncharted waters, never before sailed by civilized men, and to discover the last great tract of land that had so far eluded the bravest explorers of the times. Of the untold dangers, real or fancied, that the *Endeavor* might encounter, the worst could be a jagged rock slashing through the thin wooden hull of the ship. It did not make much difference whether or not it occurred in the dead of night, for if it happened in the cold waters of the trackless Antarctic wastes, all hands would be doomed anyway. Captain Cook carried out his orders to the letter, but on subsequent voyages he insisted on more than one ship in order to have a chance of survival in the event of disaster to the other. By way of comparison with our own age, it might be said that Captain Cook's mission demanded the same of its leader and men that an expedition to the moon would require of twentieth century explorers.

While Captain Cook contemplated his instructions, the *Endeavor* made her way to Funchal, Madeira. By the time of her arrival on September 13, she had taken on the air of a seagoing vessel. The gales and seas off Biscay had seen to that. Loose gear was stowed away, the men had gained their sea legs and had carried out their orders with dispatch. They were not so seasoned, however, that one of their most experienced men could remember that old rule of seamanship: "Never put your foot in a bight." This is a precaution to sailors of the danger of becoming entangled with a rope or hawser. On the day after the *Endeavor* arrived, master's mate Weir became entangled with the anchor buoy rope during a routine shift of anchorage, and was carried to the bottom of the harbor to his death.

Two days later the crew found out that their captain had unusual ideas about diet. While they were to live and thank him for his concern and the measures that he took to avoid an outbreak of scurvy, there must have been muttering in the forecastle on September 16 when Captain Cook punished seaman Henry Stephens and marine Thomas Dunister with twelve lashes each for refusing to take their allowance of fresh beef. This early exhibition of firmness must have convinced the crew, because there was no open opposition on the next day when the captain ordered twenty pounds of onions issued to each man of the ship's company. Two days later, on the nineteenth, Captain Cook issued another ten pounds per man, and saw to it that the onions were actually eaten and not disposed of surreptitiously.

Two days out of Funchal, Cook took another unusual step. He put the crew on three watches. It was customary for crews of sailing ships to stand "watch and watch," which gave them four hours on and four hours off, except for emergency operations when the familiar cry, "All hands on deck," brought every man to action. It was impossible for the crew to get enough sleep or take proper care of the ship during their time off. Cook reasoned that his men would be healthier and would be able to do their work better if they had more reasonable hours, more rest, warm clothes, and clean living spaces. Accordingly he set up this system of watches which permitted the crew to stand watch for four hours and have eight hours off. (With minor variations this is standard practice in most of the world's navies today.) He also required all quarters, and particularly the crew's berthing spaces, to be regularly cleaned and ventilated and scrubbed down with vinegar. These were innovations for the tough sailors on the *Endeavor* who were used to wearing dirty clothes, sleeping in wet garments, and even being punished for changing dress without permission.

When the *Endeavor* crossed the Equator en route to Brazil, Captain Cook hove to in order to observe the ancient crossing-the-line ceremony. Everyone who "could not prove upon a sea chart that he had before crossed the Line" had to either pay a bottle of rum or be ducked in the sea. The crew submitted a list of eligible victims which included even the dogs and cats. One of the crew's journals described the ceremony as follows: "At 4 hove the Ship too and the yard rope being reeved ducked 22 of the People who behaved with great spirit and gave universal satisfaction. The Evening was spent merrily without Debauch." Joseph Banks paid in brandy for himself, his servants, and his dogs. Discipline would not permit the captain to suffer a ducking, so it is presumed that Cook forfeited a bottle of rum.

At Rio de Janeiro the *Endeavor* was met with suspicion and suffered frustrating delay. The Viceroy of Brazil would not believe that Cook was on a scientific expedition, and refused to even look at his commission. During *Endeavor*'s three-week visit, the Viceroy kept the ship under guard and refused to let Joseph Banks and his party live ashore. He allowed watering and purchase of food only under the supervision of an armed party. Captain Cook was permitted to go ashore, but always in company of a Portuguese officer. The suspicious Viceroy believed that the *Endeavor* was engaged in smuggling or some other form of clandestine trade. Captain Cook restrained himself and held his temper. He could not risk detention without hazarding a delay in arriving at Tahiti in time for the transit of Venus. He and the Viceroy exchanged several official letters, which Cook had duplicated and forwarded to England on a Spanish packet. Although he could not argue or see this inconsiderate treatment righted, he sent a well-documented situation report to the Admiralty in hopes that the British navy might demand satisfaction at a later date.

In spite of official restrictions, both Mr. Banks and Dr. Solander got ashore several times, usually at night after bribing the Portuguese sentry. They brought back many local plants and shrubs for their botanical collection. However, the surgeon, who went ashore daily to buy provisions, was much more fortunate in getting acquainted in Rio de Janeiro. He learned, for example, that the ladies of Rio were inclined to toss roses from their balconies as a signal of favor to a *cabalero* on the street who caught their fancy. During his forays into the city, surgeon Monkhouse enjoyed himself immensely, and brought back several floral bouquets as evidence of his good fortune.

During the delay in leaving port, Cook was able to make a sketch of the harbor, and write out an excellent intelligence report of the city and its defenses. He concluded (and certainly must have wished for early proof of his conclusion) that five or six English ships of the line could fight past the forts and take the city.

On December 2 the *Endeavor* was fully watered and provisioned, and Captain Cook was at last able to obtain permission to shift to the outer harbor. All hands rejoiced in this first move to leave inhospitable Rio, and Mr. Banks noted in his journal the feelings of the group: "This Morn, thank God, we have got all we want from these illiterate impolite gentry so we got up our anchor and sailed. . . ." The joy of leaving was marred by the loss of a man overboard. Peter Flower, a seaman who had sailed with Cook for over five years on the Newfoundland survey, fell overboard and was drowned before the ship's boat could reach him.

Underway from the outer bay of Rio on December 7, Cook pulled clear of all fortifications and lay to off one of the islands near the harbor entrance. He sent a party ashore in a boat to cut brooms, which he had not been permitted to do while in the harbor. The boat returned to the ship the afternoon of the next day, so the *Endeavor* steered south, taking final departure from Brazil on December 8. She made excellent time in the next thirty days, traversing a little over twenty-two hundred miles to the Strait of Le Maire, which lies north and east of Cape Horn.

On the morning of January 11, *Endeavor*'s lookout sighted the coast of Tierra del Fuego, which had been given its name by Magellan because of the many native fires that he had seen on the shore. Cook noted that the land was hilly near the shore and that "the face of the country appeared green and woody, but inland are craggy mountains."

Captain Cook's orders were to round Cape Horn rather than pass through the Strait of Magellan. Passage through the Strait of Le Maire to Cape Horn was considered less hazardous and time-consuming than the tortuous route taken by Magellan. Cook noted that the doubling of Cape Horn was considered by some to be a "mighty thing" and that "others to this day prefer the Strait of Magellan." He remarked, however, that Captain Wallis in the *Dolphin* had taken three months in getting through the straits and that Commodore Byron before him had taken seven weeks and two days. It was with some satisfaction that he compared the *Endeavor*'s thirty-three days to double the Horn with the records of other voyages. This included time out for anchoring to load wood and water.

The *Endeavor* literally clawed her way through the Strait of Le Maire. After several false starts in which the ship would make some headway only to be swept back by a change in tide, Cook decided to stay close to shore and to anchor before the tide could wipe out the day's gains. On January 15 he anchored in a small cove at Staten Island on the east side of the strait. The next day he made his way across to the Bay of Success on the Tierra del Fuego side, and remained there for five days. The time was spent in loading firewood and water from the beach and stowing guns below decks in preparation for the high gales and seas of Cape Horn.

During this stop, the *Endeavor* lost two more men

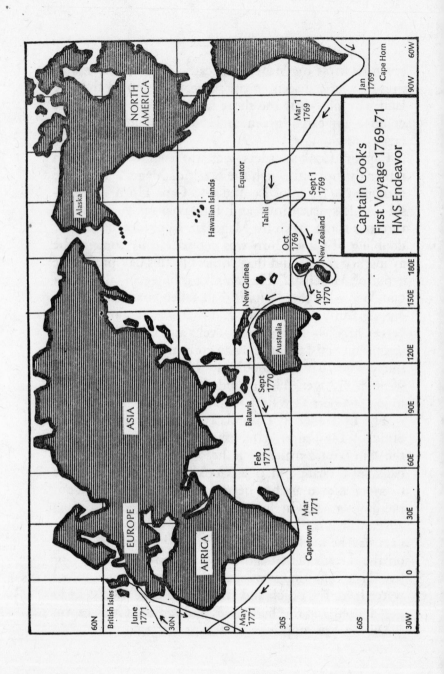

Captain Cook's
First Voyage 1769-71
HMS Endeavor

NORTH AMERICA

Alaska

Hawaiian Islands

Equator

Tahiti

Sept 1 1769

New Zealand

Oct 1769

Mar 1 1769

Jan 1769

Cape Horn

New Guinea

Australia

Apr 1770

Batavia

Sept 1770

Feb 1771

ASIA

EUROPE

AFRICA

British Isles

June 1771

Mar 1771

Capetown

May 1771

60N

30N

0

30S

60S

30W   0   30E   60E   90E   120E   150E   180E   150W   120W   90W   60W

in a foraging expedition led by Mr. Banks. The group set out on a bright, sunny morning, anticipating a splendid specimen-gathering picnic. They unexpectedly encountered a swamp which so delayed them that they could not return to the ship and had to remain in the woods overnight. The weather turned bitter cold and a blizzard set in. The group kept moving until they could find shelter and build a fire. Two of Banks's servants, whose main duty was to carry rum for the group, had imbibed so freely that they succumbed to the combination of liquor and cold. They lay down and refused to move in spite of warnings that they would die if they did not keep moving to a place of shelter.

While in the Bay of Success, the crew of the *Endeavor* had their first encounter with the natives of Tierra del Fuego. Captain Cook was disappointed, calling them, "perhaps as miserable a set of People as are this day upon Earth." Contrary to earlier reports, the Patagonians were not giants, but were a moderately sized, wretchedly backward race. The natives who, according to Byron, were eight feet tall, were nowhere to be found. The tribe at the Bay of Success lived primarily on game, which they hunted with bow and arrow, and shellfish.

Before leaving the anchorage, Captain Cook sent a party of men to gather wild celery. Having fed this in quantity to his men, prepared sailing directions for passing the Strait of Le Maire, computed the latitude, and made navigational sketches of the waters, Cook was finally ready to move on.

Comparatively good weather—not the usual giant seas and tempests found at Cape Horn—favored the *Endeavor* as she swung south and into the Pacific

Ocean. Cook kept heading south to latitude 60 degrees and then worked his way northwest, well to the westward of tracks made by other explorers.

This was characteristic of Cook, and it marked him as a great explorer. He never stuck to the beaten trail, nor was he reluctant to sail close to new shores. A later entry in his journal bares his philosophy: "Was it not for the pleasure which naturally results to a man from being the first discoverer, even was it nothing more than sand and shoals . . . The world will hardly admit of an excuse for a man leaving a coast unexplored he has once discovered . . ."

During the long stretch north, the *Endeavor* was out of sight of land. Her track passed close by Pitcairn Island, where Cook noted flights of birds, but he missed the island and pressed on to the estimated latitude of Tahiti. He reached it at a point well to the east and then "ran down the latitude" toward his target. This course led him through the Tuomotu Archipelago and various islands of the group called Society Islands. In these calm waters Cook put his crew back on a three section watch, noting that they had been on "watch and watch" since they had arrived at Tierra del Fuego.

On April 10, Tahiti loomed over the horizon, and on the thirteenth, well in time for the transit of Venus, the *Endeavor* anchored in Matavia Bay. The first important leg of the voyage was over.

CHAPTER FIVE

TAHITI, 1769

HAVING arrived in Tahiti seven weeks before the transit, Cook spent the time in making careful scientific preparations and in cultivating the natives. Actually, the natives commanded his first attention, for it was necessary to be on amicable terms with them so that his party could make the astronomical observations without disturbance. The friendly and casual Tahitians were a problem, however, for they were excited and wished to trade and satisfy their curiosity. It also was a part of their nature to steal—not for gain, necessarily, but primarily for the thrill and excitement of the chase.

Cook felt that the crew of the *Endeavor* needed firm rules for conducting business with the natives and accordingly posted the following:

RULES to be observe'd by every person in or belonging to His Majestys Bark the Endeavour, for the better establishing a regular and uniform Trade for Provisions with the Inhabitants of Georges Island.

1st To endeavour by every fair means to cultivate a friendship with the natives and to treat them with all imaginable humanity.

2nd A proper person or persons will be appointed to trade with the Natives for all manner of Provisions, fruit, and other productions of the earth; and no officer or Seaman, or other person belonging to the Ship, excepting such as are so appointed, shall Trade or offer to Trade for any sort of Provisions, Fruit, or other productions of the earth unless they have my leave so to do.

3rd   Every person employ'd a Shore on any duty what soever is strictly to attend to the same, and if by neglect he looseth any of his Arms or woorking tools, or suffers them to be stole, the full Value thereof will be charge'd against his pay according to the Custom of the Navy in such cases, and he shall recive such farther punishment as the nature of the offence may deserve.

4th   The same penalty will be inflicted on every person who is found to imbezzle, trade or offer to trade with any part of the Ships Stores of what nature soever.

5th   No Sort of Iron, or any thing that is made of Iron, or any sort of Cloth or other usefull or necessary articles are to be given in exchange for any thing but provisions.

J.C.

While these rules were generally observed, some of the men could not resist the wiles of Tahitian girls who would bestow favors for provisions, nails, or the worthless jewelry and beads which the *Endeavor* carried in great supply. Infractors who were caught were punished, but a great deal of clandestine trading—particularly in nails—existed. (At one time Cook feared that the *Endeavor* would fall apart, plank by plank, unless this practice was stopped.)

It was more difficult to exact controlled behavior from the natives. They were "prodigious expert" at thieving, which they considered a playful sport rather than something illegal. They were prepared for punishment when they were caught, and did not resent it. As an example of the Tahitians' expertise in this art, someone stole Captain Cook's stockings from beneath his head as he lay asleep in a tent ashore. By far the most serious theft was that of a quadrant which was needed for the Venus transit. Cook would not put up with such a vital loss and organized an armed party in pursuit; he informed the local chiefs of his determination to retrieve the instrument, and set out in search. Joseph Banks preceded him, however, and located the quadrant without incident, but the Tahitians had dismantled and distributed some of its parts. The quadrant was reassembled by the scientists as best they could, but its performance was never quite satisfactory thereafter. When the observations of Venus turned out to be somewhat inaccurate, Cook listed the stolen quadrant as one of the possible causes.

Cook chose a site on the eastern shore of Matavia Bay for his main observation post. This remote point, he felt, would disturb the natives least, and it could be well defended. Fort Venus was a combination observation site and armed fortification. Cook mounted six swivels and two four-pound guns in the fort and put two more four-pounders on the nearby riverbank. At all times he kept a garrison of about forty-five men equipped with small arms. As an additional precaution, he warped the *Endeavor* into a close anchorage where her guns commanded the beach approaches to the fort. Once these arrangements were completed, Cook thought himself "perfectly secure from anything these people could attempt." He now landed his scientific instruments, which consisted of an astronomical clock, a journeyman clock, the quadrant, and two telescopes.

Each piece was carefully mounted and positioned well before the time of transit.

Thus prepared, Cook and his "gentlemen" scientists were at liberty to get better acquainted with the natives, with whom there had been some trade but few social contacts. Joseph Banks proved to be very effective in his relations with the Tahitians. A bluff, gregarious young man, he traveled extensively, attended feasts, supervised most of the ship's trade, and became enraptured with the Tahitian way of life. Cook was less impulsive; because of his reticent nature, as well as his sense of responsibility, he took a more detached view of the enchanted isle. His journal contains a long description of the land, its people and their customs. Some pertinent extracts show the depth of his interest and the practical way in which he observed a society completely different from anything that he had seen before. Cook began with a geographical description.

"The island is called by the natives *Otaheite* and was first discovered by Captain Wallis in His Majesty's Ship Dolphin on the 19th of June 1767. . . ." He went on to give Wallis credit for having determined the longitude of Tahiti to ". . . within a half degree of the truth." Cook prepared sailing directions for entering Matavia Bay, and noted several other anchorages to the west. Although he listed one that is now the present harbor of Papeete, he did not recognize it as a better year-round anchorage than Matavia Bay.

Tahiti had abundant produce that needed little cultivation. Fish were available, but in view of the difficulties encountered in fishing, the natives regarded fish as a luxury and usually would not trade sea produce as readily as any other. Their tame animals were hogs, poultry, and dogs. The men of the *Endeavor* readily admitted that South Sea dog (cooked in a Tahitian stone pit) was as good as English lamb. The native diet was plain, but they spiced it with salt water, which Cook called "universal sauce." He remarked that "hardly anyone sits to a meal without a cocoanut shell full of it standing by them into which they dip most of what they eat especially fish, drinking at intervals large sups of it out of their hands, so that a man may use half a pint at a meal."

The Tahitians of Cook's time were a tall, well-proportioned people, with brown skins and black hair. The well-to-do stayed in the shade as much as possible, because fairness of skin was highly esteemed. Both sexes were graceful and extremely clean, bathing at least three times a day in fresh water. But Cook noted two disagreeable personal traits. The first was the Tahitians' habit of using scented coconut oil on their heads, and the second was their tendency to eat lice, which most of them had in abundance in their hair in spite of their baths.

When they were not eating or sleeping, Tahitians amused themselves by singing, dancing, wrestling, and shooting their bows and arrows. Cook saw one man shoot an arrow 274 yards, "yet he looked upon it as no great shot." Tahitian mores troubled Cook, who looked upon their casual lovemaking as a threat to his men's health. He found the following Tahitian custom "inhuman and contrary to the first principles of human nature."

". . . I do not expect to be believed as it is founded upon a Custom so inhuman and contrary to the first principles of human nature: it is this, that more than one half of the better sort of the inhabitants have enter'd into a resolution of injoying free liberty in love without being troubled or disturbed by its concequences; these mix and cohabit together with the utmost freedom and the Children who are so unfortunate as to be thus begot are smother'd at the moment of their birth; many of these people contract intimacies and live together as Man and Wife for years in the Course of which the Children that are born are destroy'd. They are so far from concealing it that they rather look upon it as a branch of freedom upon which they value themselves. They are call'd Arreoy's and have meetings among themselves where the men amuse themselves with wristling &ca and the women in dancing the indecent dance before mentioned in the Course of which they give full liberty to their desires but I believe keep up to the appearance of decency. I never saw one of these meetings. Dr. Munkhouse saw part of one enough to make him give credit to what we had been told.

Both sexes express the most indecent ideas in conversation without the least emotion and they delight in such conversation beyond any other. Chasity indeed is but little Valued especially among the middle people, if a wife is found guilty of a breach of it her only punishment is a beating from her husband; the men will very readily offer the young women to strangers even their own daughters and think it very strange if you refuse them but this is done meerly for the lucre of gain . . ."

One result of Tahitian promiscuity was the rapid spread of venereal disease. Cook was reasonably certain that the *Endeavor*'s crew did not bring it to the island. He wrote, "I had taken the greatest pains to discover if any of the Ships Company had the disorder upon him for above a month before our arrival here and ordered the Surgeon to examine every man the least suspected. . . ." In retrospect it seems most likely that the disease was introduced by the crews of Bougainville's ships, when they called at the island in 1768. No matter what the source had been, twenty-four seamen and nine out of eleven marines on the *Endeavor* contracted the disease. Cook was so concerned about the health of his afflicted men and their ability to withstand cold weather that he delayed his voyage southward one month, to give the men time to recover. He took his ship on a leisurely survey of the islands to the west of Tahiti, thereby removing his crew from the source of temptation and trouble.

Cook's observation of the island and its inhabitants were formed during the *Endeavor*'s entire stay at Matavia Bay. Returning to a chronological account of "remarkable occurences" as seen in Cook's journal, the next important item listed is the actual observation of the transit on June 3. The day was as favorable as the group could wish; there was not a cloud in the sky and the air was perfectly clear. However, it was oppressively hot, as indicated by a thermometer reading of 119 degrees at noon. The main observations were taken at Fort Venus, but Cook also sent two subsidiary parties to neighboring islands. Each group noted an "atmosphere or dusky shade" around the body of the planet which made it difficult to determine exact times of contact. When the data was finally examined by the Royal Astronomer after the voyage, the readings were found to be inaccurate, as were the observations made at Hudson Bay and in Norway. Subsequent observations made a century later, in 1874 and 1882, also proved unsatisfactory, so the astronomical community eventually found another means for computing the distance between the sun and the earth.

With the first mission now completed, Captain Cook's thoughts turned toward his secret instructions, which promised exploration and adventure. While his scientists tabulated the results of the transit observations, Cook and Joseph Banks, accompanied by one native, made a complete circuit of the island in one of the ship's boats. The trip took six days and covered about ninety miles. Cook prepared a "Plan or Sketch" which was "sufficient to point out the situations of the different Bays and harbours and the figure of the island." It was an excellent, rapid piece of work which surpassed anything previously done in that area.

A week after the island circuit, and shortly before the crew was to quit Fort Venus and return aboard the *Endeavor*, two marines were discovered absent. Cook reasoned that they intended to desert, but waited a day before taking steps to find them. When he learned that they had taken to the hills, each with a Tahitian "wife," he resolved to recover them at all costs. Desertion was a dangerous precedent. He hit upon a scheme that he used successfully in all of his voyages—the use of hostages. While he generally had his way and got results with this measure, it led to his own death years later on the shores of Hawaii.

Cook and his men seized several Tahitian chiefs and told them that they would be held until the two deserters were returned. The chiefs suggested that Cook send some of his men along with theirs in the search. During the evening one of the *Endeavor* search party returned and informed the Captain that the other men had been seized and disarmed by the natives. Immediately Cook sent Lieutenant Hicks with a heavily armed party to set things right. He also told the chiefs that they would suffer if any harm came to his men. These measures and threats worked; Hicks was led to his quarry and returned to the ship with the first search party and the two deserters.

Cook then released the hostage chiefs, reflecting that ". . . we are likely to leave these people in disgust with our behavior towards them, owing wholy to the folly of two of our own people."

Two days later, on June 13, after having made amends with the Tahitians, Cook got the *Endeavor* under sail. For some time before departure several of the natives had offered to go with the *Endeavor*. At Mr. Banks's urging, as well as his guarantee to subsidize and maintain the passengers in England, Cook took aboard Tupia, a Tahitian priest and chief, together with a young boy as his servant. During the three-month stay at Tahiti, Cook and his officers had been impressed by Tupia's intelligence and geographical knowledge. They felt that he would be useful as an interpreter as well as an adviser on produce, customs, and laws existing in the strange lands they hoped to find.

With gentle breezes and fair weather, the *Endeavor* embarked on the first leg of her important second mission. As soon as the ship was "shaken down" and the crew back at their familiar routine, Captain Cook punished the two marine deserters with two dozen lashes each and released them from confinement.

The survey of Cook's Society Islands (named in honor of the Royal Society) lasted a pleasant month and three weeks. The crew of the *Endeavor* regained their health and lived off "a plentiful supply" of hogs, chickens, plantains, and yams. Loaded to the gunwales with local food supplies, the *Endeavor* headed south on August 9, 1769.

CHAPTER SIX

NEW ZEALAND, 1769-1770

THE Admiralty's secret instructions enjoined Cook to "proceed to the Southward in order to make discovery of the continent afore-mentioned until you arrive in the latitude of 40°. . . ." It took the *Endeavor* twenty-four days to penetrate that far south, although Cook took time off on August 14 and 15 to inspect and circumnavigate the island of Rurutu. Lieutenant Gore, Banks, and Tupia went in by boat to look for a landing, but found none. Instead they met with hostile natives who had to be driven off with muskets. During his circuit of the island, Cook failed to find any sort of safe harbor or anchorage, so after making careful observations to fix the island's position, he headed south once more.

The weather grew increasingly windy and cold. Giant swells tossed the *Endeavor* about, and all but the most experienced sailors became sick. The winds and rain took a serious toll of the sails and rigging.

On August 28, John Radon, the boatswain's mate, "departed this life," the victim of acute alcoholism. Lieutenant Hicks said that Radon had downed three pints of rum during the night, but no one knew where he had found that much. Mr. Banks's journal gives a clue:

". . . Rayden . . . was this morn found so drunk that he had scarce any signs of life and in about an hour he expired where he could have got his liquor is a mystery which however nobody seems to enquire into probably not fairly I have more than once had occasion to congratulate myself on my prudence in not taking wine on board at Madeira as I believe I may safely say that there is not a cask on board the ship that has not been tap'd to the great dissatisfaction of the owners who in general have had the comfort to find the gentlemen honest enough not to have filled up with salt water in some cases however this was not a consideration if much comfort as many of the casks were ⅔ empty and some quite."

Historically, sailors have usually managed to find a way to tap a surreptitious drink.

Cook's journal entry for Saturday, September 2, showed the *Endeavor* in latitude 39° 45' south and longitude 145° 39' west. The captain had not seen the least sign of land, so he reluctantly stood to the north for better weather, "lest we should receive such damages in our sails and rigging as might hinder the further prosecutions of the voyage."

His crew welcomed this change of course. On the day before, Parkinson had written: ". . . we had hard piercing gales and squalls from the W. and N.W. with violent showers of hail and rain. The sea ran mountain-high and tossed the ship upon the waves: she rolled so much we could get no rest, or scarcely lie in bed, and almost every moveable on board was thrown down and rolled about from place to place. In brief, a person, who has not been in a storm at sea, cannot form an adequate idea of the situation we were in." Despite the storm Cook felt no immediate danger, for he knew the capabilities of his craft. After the voyage, his report

53

to the Admiralty included great detail on the seaworthiness and sailing characteristics of the *Endeavor*. With regard to safety in bad weather, Cook stated that "No sea can hurt her laying to under a Main Sail or Mizon [mizzen] ballanc'd." On occasion he did just that, but in the gales at 40 degrees south latitude he was more interested in seeking calmer waters and pressing on to the west for the second mission given him by the Admiralty. In the event he failed to find the continent on the leg south to latitude 40 degrees, he recalled that he was "to proceed in search of it to the Westward between the Latitude afore mentioned and the Latitude of 35° until you discover it, or fall in with the Eastern side of . . . New Zealand."

Endeavor's track to the west lay generally within the boundaries described, except for small deviations caused when contrary winds forced her to the north. After five weeks of steady sailing, one of the youngsters on the *Endeavor*, Nicholas Young, sighted land, which was promptly named Young Nick's Head in his honor. Two days later, on October 9, Cook anchored in what he originally planned to call Endeavor Bay but called Poverty Bay "because it afforded us no one thing we wanted."

The six-month period from October, 1769, to March, 1770, was spent in exploring the coasts of New Zealand. Prior to Cook's arrival, New Zealand existed only as a point on the map where Tasman had touched one hundred and twenty-seven years before. The geographical community had accepted his theory that it was perhaps the northwestern tip of the unknown continent. Cook's thorough circumnavigation of the island group blasted this concept once and for all.

The rapidity of his circuit would not permit him to chart the coastline with exact accuracy. It had taken five years for Cook to do a thorough job of the Newfoundland coast, and New Zealand was a bigger task. Nevertheless, he did produce an outline sketch which was hailed by the British hydrographer Admiral Wharton as having "astonishing accuracy." History has shown that he made a few errors of omission and interpretation in his sweep over the twenty-four hundred miles of coastline. For example, distance or poor visibility caused him to name a piece of land Banks Island, while it was in reality joined with the mainland and is now known as Banks Peninsula.

Wharton went on to praise Cook as follows: "Never has a coast been so well laid down by a first explorer, and it must have required unceasing vigilance and continual observation, in fair weather and foul, to arrive at such a satisfactory conclusion; and with such a dull sailer as the *Endeavor* was, the six and a half months occupied in the work must be counted as a short interval in which to do it."

Cook found the warlike Maoris of New Zealand another hurdle to overcome. Unlike the friendly, fun-loving Tahitians, the Maoris were hostile and were disposed to eating opponents whom they killed in battle. On some occasions they manifested their hostility openly, lying off in their canoes at a safe distance from the *Endeavor* and taunting the Englishmen with "Come ashore and fight us and we will eat you." At other times they would appear to be friendly solely to lure a small party to an isolated beach, where they would turn on them in savage fury.

The Admiralty had foreseen the problems inherent

in meeting strange people and had entered into the instructions the following passage: "You are likewise to observe the genius, temper, disposition and number of the Natives, if there be any, and endeavor by all proper means to cultivate a friendship and alliance with them." The practical admirals had also admonished Cook with the added caution that he should take care "not to suffer yourself to be surprised by them, but to be always upon your guard against any Accident."

Even with the Tahitians, Cook's trigger-happy men had used firearms to settle a dispute. Once at Fort Venus, Midshipman Monkhouse had ordered his sentries to fire at a group of Tahitians who had made off with a musket. Parkinson heard the shots and came upon the scene to find the men firing "with the greatest glee imaginable, as if they had been shooting at wild ducks." The *Endeavor*'s crew had more provocation with the Maoris, and were further inspired to defend themselves against the real possibility that they might be eaten. Cook gradually worked out a practical routine which proved to be fairly successful. He used what is now called a "graduated response," which had several options. For example, he would use the ship's guns fired wide to intimidate by noise and to demonstrate the ability to throw a charge farther than the natives could hurl rocks and spears. The superiority of the ship's guns was obvious. For closer encounters Cook would warn the Maoris off with small shot (bird shot, used to kill ducks). The natives soon learned to appreciate that Cook used this superiority only to demonstrate, not to kill, and realized that he would resort to the deadly musket ball only as a last resort.

His vigilance in these matters paid off. He protected

his men and gradually arrived at a workable coexistence with the Maoris. At least he avoided the fate which later fell to Captain Furneaux during the second voyage. At Queen Charlotte Sound an altercation with the natives flared up in violence, and the Maoris massacred an entire boat crew of the ship *Adventure*.

The details of the *Endeavor*'s circuit of New Zealand are interesting, and they reveal the stature and determination of her captain.

Poverty Bay was a disappointment. During the two-day stay, Cook's men found neither wood nor fresh water, and had to kill three or four natives in self-defense. They took three youths prisoner and brought them aboard the ship. There the young men were treated with kindness and when they finally realized that they were not going to be eaten the surprised Maoris became "as cheerful and as merry as if they had been with their own friends." As a matter of fact, Cook had difficulty in getting rid of them when he sailed from Poverty Bay.

Cook chose to head south down the New Zealand coast, intending to go as far as latitude 40 or 41 degrees south, and then turn northward if he found nothing to encourage him to proceed farther. During the first part of this leg, they saw an island that reminded them of home and the English Channel. Cook nostalgically named it the Isle of Portland for its resemblance to Portland, England. Just beyond this island the shore bent inland to form a large bay which he named Hawke's Bay in honor of Sir Edward Hawke, First Lord of the Admiralty. The southern extremity of the bay received the picturesque name "Cape Kidnappers" as a result of the following incident:

Some fishing boats came alongside the *Endeavor* and sold the crew some "stinking fish." Cook noted that one of the natives wore a black skin which looked like a bear's skin, and wanted it in order to "be a better judge of what sort of an animal the first owner was." The man offered to trade for a piece of red cloth, but once having the cloth in his hands, he made off from the ship without delivering up the skin. After a short time he came back with another fishing boat to sell some more fish. At this point young Tiata, Tupia's servant, was over the side and the natives promptly seized him and dragged him into their canoe. Cook ordered his men to fire into the boat with care, brought the *Endeavor* to, and lowered a boat into the water to give chase. The firing had its effect, killing three natives and causing enough excitement to permit Tiata to jump overboard and swim to the *Endeavor*'s boat. From previous brushes with the natives, Cook had little doubt that the Maoris would have eaten Tiata if they had gotten away with him.

From Cape Kidnappers, Cook headed south, charting as he went. He drew from his earlier experience off the coasts of Newfoundland to establish a routine for quick exploration and accurate mapping. He kept a good navigational record of the *Endeavor*'s track, and probed the water's depth consistently. His leadsmen sounded the bottom at regular intervals while the watch took bearings of prominent points of land. To speed the process, Cook would send out his ship's boats to investigate beaches at closer range, to probe into coves and inlets, and to check the water's depth.

When the natives were agreeable, Cook would purchase food, and would send in parties to gather water, wood, and fresh fruit and vegetables. There were several edible wild vegetables available for his antiscorbutic diet, but he favored wild celery, which he served boiled "to the people" as regularly as he could.

At Cape Turnagain, Cook decided to reverse course and move to the north, where the promise of warmer climate and unknown land beckoned him. As he traversed his old track he conducted a more thorough exploratory sweep into Hawke's Bay, swung by Poverty Bay once again, and eagerly looked for an anchorage where there would be wood and fresh water. On October 24, the *Endeavor* anchored in Tolaga Bay, where not only was there good water and wood aplenty but also the friendliest natives so far encountered.

After a restful five-day pause in Tolaga Bay, the ship sailed around East Cape, and on November 9 arrived at Mercury Bay, where Cook and Green landed to observe the transit of Mercury across the sun's face. The friendliness of the natives encouraged some of the officers to form foraging parties inland. The land abounded with game, fresh water, celery, scurvy grass, and large trees. A brisk trade was carried on with the natives, upon whom Captain Cook made a deep impression. An early history of New Zealand, published almost a century after Cook's visit, contains an interesting account of an old Maori, who as a child had met Cook: "There was one supreme man in that ship," the old man said. "We knew that he was the lord of the whole by his perfect gentlemanly and noble demeaner. He seldom spoke, but some of the goblins [English] spoke much. But this man did not utter many words: all that he did was to handle our mats, hold our spears and clubs and touch the hair of our heads. He was a very good man, and came to us—the children—and patted our heads." Another native described him as "a noble man—cannot be lost in a crowd."

The *Endeavor* pushed north during the months of November and December, and was blown out of sight of land by a wild December gale, "which," Cook wrote, "for its strength and continuance was such as I was hardly in before." Noting a long sea swell from the west, which could only build up after travel over a wide expanse of sea, Cook reasoned that he had passed the northern tip of New Zealand and was well into the open sea. Accordingly, he returned and identified landmarks noted by Abel Tasman in his brief visit a century and a quarter before. Continuing down the west side on southerly headings, he found that in contrast to the fertile eastern shore, this western side consisted of desolate sand dunes and high mountains. At Queen Charlotte Sound, which he reached in the middle of January, Cook found an ideal place to careen his ship and clean off the barnacles and sea growth. This long inlet was named Ship Cove; it became one of Cook's favorite spots, and one which he sought out during his later voyages.

Cook climbed a high hill and determined that Ship Cove bordered a strait between the two main islands of the New Zealand group. He confirmed his ideas with a local Maori chief, and set out in February to navigate the strait, which now bears his name. After a narrow escape from treacherous currents, Cook sailed north to his familiar Cape Turnagain in order to convince his officers and Mr. Banks that they had completely circumnavigated North Island. "I then called the officers upon deck," he wrote, "and asked them whether they were not now satisfied that this land was an island, to which they answered in the affirmative. . . ."

Thus satisfied, Cook turned south once more and began a clockwise survey around South Island. At Banks Island (later renamed Banks Peninsula), Lieutenant Gore thought he saw land to the southeast. The thorough Cook pushed ahead in that direction to be sure, but after two days' chase out to sea, he returned to Banks Island and resumed the coastal survey.

In late February another gale drove the *Endeavor* out of sight of land. Cook returned after a week's delay spent weathering the storm and beating his way back to a familiar landmark, which he had named Cape Saunders. Continuing to the lowest point of New Zealand, he had a narrow escape from submerged rocks which he aptly called The Traps "because they lay as such to catch unwary strangers." Rounding the southernmost point of Stewart Island, which he named South Cape, the *Endeavor* ran head on into another storm. This one also took her out of sight of land, and once more the Captain stubbornly brought her back to pick up the same trail. He was gratified to see the coast turn unmistakably northward, which eliminated all doubt—New Zealand was not a continent but two great islands, similar to the sketches which the Maori chiefs had drawn.

In a little over two weeks, the *Endeavor* followed the remaining part of New Zealand's west coast. Cook readily pointed out that bad weather had forced him to skip a detailed observation of twenty-five miles of coastline, but he quickly added that, even so, "the mountains inland were visible enough." These rugged mountains, he wrote, "are of a prodigious height and appear to consist of nothing but barren rocks, covered in many places with large patches of snow which perhaps have laid there since creation. No country upon earth can appear with a more rugged and barren aspect than this doth from the sea. . . ."

On March 27 the circumnavigation of New Zealand was completed, and the *Endeavor* anchored once more near Queen Charlotte Sound. By this tremendous accomplishment, James Cook gave England an undisputed claim to a large new country. Although Abel Tasman had first seen the west coast of New Zealand, he had never landed on it, probably because, as Cook put it, "he was discouraged from it by the natives killing 3 or 4 of his people at the first and only place he anchored at." Cook's masterful survey produced an outline chart that has stood up through the ages. Details have been filled in, and a few corrections have been added here and there. As for his own opinion, Cook thought that "The situation of few parts of the world are better determined than these Islands are, being settled by some hundreds of observations of the Sun and Moon and one by the transit of Mercury. . . ."

First corroboration came from French explorer Crozet who visited New Zealand shortly after Cook: "As soon as I obtained information of the voyage of the Englishman, I carefully compared the chart I had prepared of that part of the coast of New Zealand along which we had coasted with that prepared by Captain Cook and his officers. I found it of an exactitude and of a thoroughness of detail which astonished me beyond all powers of expression, and I doubt much whether the charts of our own French coasts are laid down with greater precision. I think therefore that I cannot do better than to lay down our track off New Zealand on the chart prepared by this celebrated navigator."

As he had done at Tahiti, Cook wrote an extensive account of the terrain and natives of New Zealand. It was characteristic of the man, who knew that Maoris gave no quarter to enemies, and in most cases ate their victims, that he described them sympathetically. Underneath their war paint and tattoos he discerned that "they appear to be of a gentle disposition and treat each other with utmost kindness and are as modest and reserved in their behavior and conversation as the most polite nations of Europe. . . . Notwithstanding their custom of eating their enemies, the circumstances and temper of these people is in favor of those who might settle among them as a colony." History has proven Cook right in this, emphasizing again that he was perhaps one hundred years ahead of his time.

Cook's brilliant achievement included volumes of information which proved that New Zealand was ideal for European settlement. A great deal of the soil was rich, and in the northern part there was an abundance of fish and good timber. It was a fertile, beautiful land, in which industrious colonists could find both a haven and new horizons.

CHAPTER SEVEN

THE
GREAT BARRIER REEF

WITH the exploration of New Zealand behind him, Cook had checked off each of the Admiralty's instructions except the last one. This was to return to England "either around the Cape of Good Hope or Cape Horn, as from circumstances you may judge the Most Eligible way of returning home."

The route via Cape Horn was attractive. Winds were generally from the west, which promised good sailing, and the route would take them through the one promontory of the unexplored South Pacific that lay between the *Endeavor*'s track from Cape Horn to Tahiti and the southern thrust that she had made from Tahiti to latitude 40 degrees south. Referring to the southern continent as "real or imaginary," Cook pointed out that "there is left a small space to the northward of 40° where the Grand Object can lay, I think it would be a great pitty that this thing which at times has been the object of many ages and Nations should not now be wholly cleared up. . . ." No land that lay to the south of either Cape Horn or the southern tip of New Zealand could be worthy of great hopes, for it would be as barren, cold, and uninviting as Tierra del Fuego or the Falkland Islands. But undiscovered land north of the fortieth parallel was worth finding.

Despite the attractions of this alternate route, Cook turned it down in view of practical disadvantages. First, he would have to sail through those rough waters in the middle of antarctic winter with sails and rigging that were all but spent. Second, the *Endeavor*'s bottom was weakened from a year and a half of continuous sailing, a great deal of it in tropical waters where sea worms did their greatest damage. Also his supply of staple food had diminished to about four months' rations. The route offered no places to refit or to obtain water, provisions, and wood.

This persuaded him to choose a westward passage via the Cape of Good Hope. Here again he had to make a choice. He could sail south of New Holland, reversing the track of Tasman, or he could work north to Batavia and then take the familiar trade route through the Indian Ocean to Good Hope. Rejecting the southern route below New Holland as one which offered little chance of new discoveries, Cook decided to return via Batavia, but in a different way than had ever before been attempted. This decision permitted him to explore the fertile eastern coast of Australia, which some scholars claim was his greatest discovery. At any rate, it gave England an undisputed claim to the largest remaining unexplored continent.

On April 1, the men of the *Endeavor* had their last look at New Zealand and took departure from a prominent point which they named Cape Farewell. The route chosen, wrote Cook, was "to steer to the Westward until we fall in with East Coast of New Holland

and then to follow the direction of that Coast to the northward or what other direction it may take until we arrive at its Northern extremity, and if this should be found impractical then to endeavor to fall in with the lands or islands discovered by Quiros."

Had Cook foreseen the danger of this route he would never have followed it. In retrospect, after he had once transited the Great Barrier Reef, he wrote, "Coasted the shore to the Northward through the most dangerous navigation that perhaps ever ship was in." This, from the fearless Cook, was a warning indeed to all other mariners.

The Tasman Sea is known today as one of the roughest bodies of water in the world. The *Endeavor* ran through gales, squalls, and tempestuous seas for two weeks before Cook sensed that land was ahead. While his men attributed his ability to "feel" land to almost superhuman or magical powers, it was an acquired ability which he drew from his powers of observation and knowledge of the sea. Cook had learned that the long, hollow swells of the South Pacific required great open reaches of ocean in order to build up. Among other signs, he recognized certain sea birds as those of limited range, and he could distinguish some types of sea growth as those which were found near coastlines. For two nights before he sighted land, he would lie to, or tack back and forth over water that he had covered during daylight. Finally, on April 19, Lieutenant Hicks sighted land; he thus became the first European to set eyes on the eastern coast of New Holland, which, since 1817, has been known officially as Australia.

Cook named this promontory Point Hicks in honor of the lieutenant, and he eagerly steered for the coast.

With his dwindling supply of staples aboard, Cook decided to make a fairly rapid transit northward, sketching in the bare outline of the coast. In doing this, he sailed from point to point, landing when he needed water and fresh food, but passing up many inlets and bays which he would have liked to explore more thoroughly. This procedure caused him to sail past one of the world's greatest natural harbors, Port Jackson, where the city of Sydney was founded in 1788.

For a week after sighting land, the *Endeavor* sailed northward, searching for a decent harbor and fresh water. On April 29 the ship anchored in her first Australian port, which yielded so many botanical specimens for Banks's collection that Cook named it Botany Bay. Here the men of the *Endeavor* found a new kind of native. These aborigines were by far the most backward that they had encountered. Unlike the Maoris, they could not understand Tupia, nor were they intelligent. Completely naked and living a substandard existence in miserable huts, they made a stout and defiant but short defense and then melted into the undergrowth.

Cook departed from Botany Bay on May 7 and made good time to the north. By the twenty-third he had passed Moreton Bay, where the city of Brisbane is now located, and put in at another bay which he named Bustard Bay in honor of a large bird that Banks shot for the wardroom table. There they found fresh water, but noted that in this semitropical climate the land was more arid and the soil was thin and sandy. Sailing north again he had difficulty finding fresh water in the forbidding shoreline, and spent two days in an unsuccessful search. Appropriately naming this area Thirsty Sound, he sailed day and night to make better time. In doing so, he unknowingly entered one of the most dangerous bodies of water known to man. For one thousand miles the Australian mainland is paralleled by the Great Barrier Reef, which is dotted with jagged rocks, low sandy inlets, razor-sharp coral reefs, and treacherous currents. At high tide a great part of the reef is just under water.

Cook and his men sensed the danger. The *Endeavor*'s progress slowed to a crawl as she inched her way through tortuous passages. Often it was necessary to have the ship's boat lead the way, probing for a channel devoid of coral pinnacles. Leadsmen were kept in the chains, taking soundings with monotonous regularity. A watch was posted by the anchor in instant readiness to let go when danger neared.

On the night of June 10 the bottom showed an unevenness which sounded a warning. Cook ordered all men to their stations, but when the danger seemed past, all except the night watch turned in. Cook was in his cabin when disaster struck. Without warning, the *Endeavor* piled up on a coral pinnacle and began beating against it.

From this time until the *Endeavor* was clear of the reef twenty-three hours later, Cook's journal is a dispassionate listing of the desperate efforts that a masterful seaman took to extricate his ship. It was like Cook not to enter anything about his own personal courage or the steadying influence that his calm manner and efficiency had on his crew. The situation was ripe for panic, but Banks noted that the commander was instantly upon decks clad only "in his drawers . . . and gave his orders with his wonted coolness and precision."

Centuries of experience in shipwrecks had taught professional seamen the practical essentials of getting a grounded ship clear. Cook's procedures would meet with approbation before any court of inquiry. He furled all sails and immediately took soundings around the ship to determine the best direction for getting clear. Noting that the *Endeavor* had unfortunately grounded at high tide, he determined to have all in readiness for the next high water. He started his men pumping water that had leaked through the hole, put out his boats, and proceeded to lighten ship. The small boats carried out anchors to strategic points for hauling the ship off. Other crewmen busily went to work throwing over ballast, guns, stores, and even some fresh water, making the ship lighter by forty to fifty tons.

At 11 A.M., high tide lacked one foot of bringing the *Endeavor* clear. There was nothing to be done but wait for the night tide. Cook wrote, "We had now no hope but from the tide at midnight, and this only founded on the generally received opinion amongst seamen, that the night tide rises higher than the day tide." As the flood tide came in, the *Endeavor* righted, and more water poured into the ship's hold. It was "an alarming and I may say terrible Circumstance and threatened immediate destruction to us as soon as the ship was afloat." Nevertheless, he could not see any future in remaining high on the coral reef. The weather at the moment was calm, but all hands knew that the *Endeavor* would break into pieces with the first fresh gale. The preparatory measures paid off. Shortly before 10 P.M., with mighty hauling and pumping, the men of the *Endeavor* pulled her free, and anchored safely in deep water.

Now it became a battle against the leak. If the pumps could not stay ahead of the water that poured through the *Endeavor*'s wound, the ship would be doomed. After holding their own by means of uninterrupted pumping at which all hands took a turn—even Cook and Banks—the crew fashioned a mat out of sail and oakum and hauled it across the ship's holed bottom. This reduced the flow of water and the *Endeavor*'s tired men were now able to maintain headway with only one pump.

In these trying circumstances the wisdom of Cook's choice of a shallow draft collier "capable of bearing the ground" was proven. The *Endeavor* had to be repaired, and the only means available was to beach her in a sheltered harbor. Cook found a place by a river, now called Endeavor River, and carefully brought his wounded ship into safe harbor. There they put some of the crew ashore and lightened the forward part of the ship sufficiently to haul her up on the bank at high water. In this position the holes were exposed at low tide so that the carpenters could make repairs. Inspection of the bottom showed that the coral pinnacle had made a clean cut, and, providentially, a large piece of coral had wedged itself into the hole. Had it not been for this, the *Endeavor* would surely have sunk when she was pulled off the reef.

It took six weeks to patch the bottom and wait for a spring tide that would refloat the ship. Cook gave his men considerable freedom, particularly at high water when little work could be accomplished on the hull. They fished, caught turtles, and conducted short surveying trips. Banks and Gore went hunting and bagged their first kangaroo. During this entire episode Banks was amazed at the performance of the ship's crew. Impressed sailors who suffered through the stern discipline of the British navy had earned very poor reputations for efficiency in times of disaster. In other cases of shipwreck, crews had gotten irresponsibly drunk, or had turned on their officers in an insane rage. Yet Cook turned this disaster into another adventure. He refused to despair or even consider failure. Even though they were shipwrecked on an unknown coast and had jettisoned many supplies and guns that were badly needed, even with the first signs of scurvy among the crew, the fear of the natives, and memories of the cannibalistic Maoris, the motley crew of the *Endeavor* never questioned Cook's authority or failed to support him. It was an acid test of command, not seamanship, and Cook passed it with flying colors.

At Endeavor River, Cook made his first successful contact with Australian natives. Since his previous offers of friendship had been refused by the shy savages, he tried another tactic—indifference. Gradually, curiosity consumed the natives and they ventured into the camp. In the weeks that followed they became friendly and were constantly in camp or aboard ship. This relationship, however, was marred by an unusual occurrence. One day the native visitors aboard the *Endeavor* tried to carry off a large sea turtle that the men had caught for food. When they were prevented from doing this, the angry nomads dashed ashore and set fire to the dry grass that surrounded the camp. It immediately became a roaring fire, threatening tents, fishnets, and ship's supplies. Only with heroic fire fighting were Cook and his men able to save their establishment. Yet, after it was over, Cook pursued the natives, and instead of punishing them, made peace, which he cemented with small gifts.

On August 6, Cook took the *Endeavor* out of the river and resumed his search for a strait that would lead him to Batavia. Time was an important factor because the November monsoon in that area would bring unfavorable winds and delay the *Endeavor*'s progress west. With food running low, and several small leaks still causing considerable trouble, Cook resolved to make the best possible time. He found a narrow channel through the barrier reef and enjoyed three days' sailing in the open sea. It was a relief and, for the first time in one thousand miles, the *Endeavor* was able to take leadsmen out of the chains and cease taking continuous soundings. It was a short-lived respite; soon the ship faced a danger even greater than Endeavor Reef.

One of Cook's reasons for coasting the shore of Australia was to determine if its northern part ended with a strait or joined New Guinea as a single landmass. Accordingly, even though he had the *Endeavor* in the open sea, he did not sail very far away from land, remaining in the water just outside of the barrier reef. On August 16, the *Endeavor* was a respectable distance from the reef when the wind shifted to the east. Cook tacked back and forth in a desperate attempt to get clear, but when the wind died he was closer to the reef than before. As he wrote it, "A little after 4 o'clock the roaring of the Surf was plainly heard, and at day break the vast foaming breakers were too plainly to be seen not a Mile from us towards which we found the ship was carried by the waves surprising fast." The water was too deep for anchoring, so the ship's boats were put out to tow the ship into a position near an opening through the reef. But the small boats could make little headway. By six o'clock the *Endeavor* was eighty to one hundred yards from the breakers, and was only the width of one wave from destruction. In retrospect Cook felt that "all the dangers we had escaped were little in comparison of being thrown upon this reef where the ship must be dashed to pieces in a moment. A reef such as is here spoke of is scarcely known in Europe, it is a wall of Coral Rock rising all most perpendicular out of the unfathomable Ocean . . . the large waves . . . make a most terrible surf breaking mountains high."

Fortunately, with the help of a friendly breeze and desperate work by the ship's boats, the *Endeavor* slowly managed to pull clear; finally an ebb tide raced through the channel, pushing her a mile out to sea. Cook sent Lieutenant Hicks out in the longboat to probe for another opening. One was found, and the *Endeavor* entered it during flood tide on August 17. Cook described it as a "mill race," and named the opening Providential Channel.

Returning to the familiar sounding and probing along the coast, Cook moved north through dangers seldom encountered since. At the tip of York Cape, the coastline tapered off to the west, and Cook knew that he had finally completed his transit of the Australian coast. On August 21 he took a party of men with him to a small island, which he named Possession Island, and took possession of the entire east coat from latitude 10° 30' south to Point Hicks in New South Wales, in the name of King George III. Afterward the party fired three volleys of small arms and cheered three times, "which was answered from the ship."

The *Endeavor* then made her way through Endeavor Strait into the open water of Torres Strait, and on

73

August 29 fell in with the coast of New Guinea. This achievement gave Cook the satisfaction of proving that "New Holland [Australia] and New Guinea are two separate lands or islands, which until this day hath been a doubtful point with geographers."

This remarkable voyage, which produced an outline map of two thousand miles of Australian coast, had been completed in a little over four months in the face of tremendous difficulties. Weary and spent, the *Endeavor* headed for Batavia and rest.

CHAPTER EIGHT

BATAVIA AND HOME

AFTER the passage of Torres Strait, Cook's first voyage of discovery was essentially over. True, the *Endeavor* was a long way from England, but there was no longer the thrill of discovery or the necessity to chart new coasts. There remained, however, the hazards of shipwreck and of storms in a tired ship, and, perhaps worst of all, there were the hazards of civilization.

During their two years aboard the *Endeavor*, the men had followed a strict regimen and diet. Due to this they were unusually healthy. At the same time, however, they had lost some of the natural immunities which men normally acquire through years of living in crowded cities. Unwittingly, the *Endeavor* sailed into Batavia during a particularly bad season of malaria and dysentery. For the men aboard the *Endeavor* it turned out to be a city of death. Cook called it "the land that kills." In a very short time, three-fourths of the crew fell ill. By November only twelve men could be mustered for duty. Banks and Solander were stricken and escaped serious illness by a narrow margin. With Banks's fortune to fall back upon, they took an unusual cure. Each bought a Malay woman and retired to the hills in the country, "hoping that the tenderness of the sex

75

would prevail even here, which indeed we found it to do."

Many good men who should have had the pleasure of recounting their South Sea adventures in London pubs died either in Batavia or on the next leg home. Batavia claimed seven, among them the Tahitians, Tupia and his servant. Twenty-three more were buried at sea on the voyage home, among them Green, the astronomer; Parkinson, the artist; Lieutenant Hicks; Molyneux, the master; Monkhouse, the surgeon, and Monkhouse's brother Jonathan, the midshipman Cook trusted so much. It was a terrible blow to Cook who had fought so long to protect his wards from scurvy, and who had written proudly on his arrival at Batavia, "I have the satisfaction to say that I have not lost one man by sickness during the whole voyage." Up to that time he had lost only eight, mostly by accident.

The ship itself was the only thing to profit from the visit to Batavia. Dutch and Javanese shipwrights gave her a thorough overhaul and new sails. Cook had hardly been ready for the revealing inspection on November 9. They careened the ship and found the hull in an amazing condition. The false keel was gone, the main keel "was wounded in many places very considerably," and much of the sheathing was off. Two planks, six feet long, were within one eighth of an inch of being cut through. The main timbers, Cook wrote, had been so eaten through by sea worms that "it was a matter of surprise to everyone who saw her bottom how we had kept her above water, and yet in this condition we had sailed some hundreds of leagues in as dangerous a Navigation as in any part of the world, happy in being ignorant of the continual danger we were in." Cook must have reflected on his good fortune to have rejected the option of sailing from New Zealand to England via Cape Horn. In those rough seas the *Endeavor*'s hull would have undoubtedly given way, ending in disaster what has been called the most successful voyage of discovery in all history.

On the day after Christmas, 1770, Cook got all of the sick aboard and moved to an anchorage in the roads. When the wind was favorable, on December 27, he sailed for the Cape of Good Hope, noting that everyone was either sick or in a weakened condition—with one exception. This was the sailmaker, "an old man of 70 or 80 years of age" who had been "generally more or less drunk every day."

The *Endeavor* carried the seeds of death with her. The water kegs were filled with amoeba-poisoned water, and hordes of mosquitoes thrived in damp pockets of the ship's hold. Fever and dysentery stayed with the ship until it reached South Africa. John Ravenhill, the old sailmaker, was deprived of his inexhaustible source of liquor, and finally succumbed on January 27. It is interesting to note that this man, whom Cook described as "an old man of 70 or 80 years" was actually only forty-nine. Apparently his years of incontinence had not been kind to him.

The melancholy voyage to the Cape of Good Hope was marked by the splash of bodies buried at sea. Cook's scientific mind vainly sought for an explanation. A poignant journal entry showed his frustration: "It is to be wished for the Good of all Seamen and Mankind in General that some preventative was found out against this disease and put in practice when it is common, for it is impossible to victual and water a ship in those climates but what some one Article or another, according to different people's opinion, must have been the means of bringing on the flux." Cook had conquered scurvy with imagination and determination, but in this he had benefited from earlier investigations and tests which isolated scurvy as a deficiency disease. He and the rest of the world would have to wait for Louis Pasteur and Robert Koch to learn about the conquering of harmful bacteria. Meanwhile, Batavia and other malaria-ridden ports in the tropics continued to take their toll of seamen, who seemed to be particularly susceptible to infection.

The men of the *Endeavor* became so despondent that, in Cook's words, "no sooner was a man taken with it [disease] that he looked upon himself as dead." One man, who had miraculously remained in good health and had nursed the sick, came up on deck one morning and felt himself "a little griped." He immediately began to stamp his feet and shout, "I have got the gripes, I have got the gripes, I shall die, I shall die." He continued to rave until he fell into a fit and was carried off to sick bay, where, to his surprise, he quickly recovered.

In Cape Town, Cook landed his sick, took on fresh meat and greens, and emptied the slimy water kegs. The fresh winds and healthy climate of South Africa had a remarkable curative effect. When the *Endeavor* sailed after a month's stay, her crew was healthy once again.

It was now April, 1771, and the *Endeavor* was plodding the last weary leg toward England. Cook stopped at St. Helena to replenish, and joined a British convoy there for the trip back home. But, so spent were the *Endeavor*'s sails and masts that she was unable to keep up. Eventually, she had to drop out of formation and go it alone. On July 13, nearly three years after her departure, the *Endeavor* reached England and anchored in the Downs, a short distance from Dover. Cook left the ship immediately for London to make his report and rejoin his family.

The Admiralty was overwhelmed; never had an explorer submitted so much material, nor had a ship brought back so much valuable scientifically cataloged specimens of flora and fauna. True, Cook had been given definite instructions, and the *Endeavor* had carried an unusually gifted party of observers, but they had still returned with so many contributions that it would take the Admiralty and the Royal Society years of study to evaluate them all.

It was immediately evident to the scientific and naval communities that James Cook was an uncommon man. His abiding passion for work had infused everyone on the *Endeavor* with a desire to discover, to observe, and to record. His charts of over five thousand miles of coastline, a monumental work, were the result of teamwork and incessant industry. With amazing accuracy he had fixed the position of his discoveries. He had taken a few vague strips of coast and left for posterity a clear outline brilliantly defined and firmly established as territories of the British Empire. No war had given England as much as had this peaceful voyage.

It was only years later that Cook's journals were truly appreciated as veritable treasure troves of information. Anthropologists often cite them as inquisitive, intelligent first records of native peoples, their habits and customs. There for any sailor or doctor to observe were instructions for the prevention of scurvy. Young aspiring naval officers could study these pages to learn a new approach to leadership. For Cook had led his men for three years—through one of the most trying voyages of all time—with a minimum of discipline. His authority was never questioned. Hydrographers found in his journals statements of winds and seas and locations of rocks and shoals, together with calm, reassuring directions for sailing around them. Even today, the official sailing directions of these coasts sound much like Cook's journals.

In his modest way James Cook reported to the Admiralty that "the discoveries made in this voyage are not great." Yet, he continued, "I flatter myself that they are such as may merit the Attention of their Lordships, and altho' I have failed in discovering the so much talked of Southern Continent (which perhaps do not exist) . . . I presume this voyage will be found as compleat as any before made to the South Seas. . . ."

It was true that many were disappointed in his failure to discover Terra Australis Incognita. Alexander Dalrymple, who saw his pet theories retreating in the light of brilliant discovery, remained Cook's enemy to his death; he studied the *Endeavor*'s voyages with great care, hoping to find some point of omission that he could criticize. Maskelyne, the Royal Astronomer, found fault with the observations of the transit of Venus. While history has shown that all of the observations of Venus taken that year were vitiated by distortion, Maskelyne was brutally critical of Green's work, even though the unfortunate man was dead and could not defend himself. Maskelyne's remark that Green's readings showed lack of care or skill drew a strong retort from Cook, who knew only too well the infinite pains to which Green had gone to obtain accuracy.

Despite those few discordant echoes, the voyage was considered a tremendous success. Three weeks after his return, the Admiralty sent Cook an official acknowledgment, which, with characteristic British understatement, contained the following good news: ". . . I have the pleasure to acquaint you that their Lordships extremely well approve of the whole of your proceedings."

Suddenly Cook became famous. His name was on everyone's lips in the coffeehouses of London. He met the First Lord of the Admiralty, the Earl of Sandwich, who was so impressed with him that he never denied anything that Cook requested in later years. This in itself was remarkable, because the Earl of Sandwich was notorious for channeling navy funds to his own personal use. The Earl informed Cook that he was to have an audience with the King and that he was to be promoted to the rank of commander.

Unselfishly, Cook commended his entire crew, and recommended several of the noncommissioned officers, including the marine corporal who had deserted, for commissioned rank.

Close students of Cook's first voyage have observed an unusual individual growth in the man himself. When he left England in 1768, Cook was just one of many experienced seamen in the British navy. He was also a first-rate coastal surveyor and a self-taught mathematician, but he had commanded only small ships and his experience was somewhat limited. His intellectual growth, spurred on by daily contacts with minds like

Banks, Solander, Green, and the other "gentlemen" aboard the *Endeavor*, was remarkable. When he returned he was not only a great commander, weathered in adversity and confident in his abilities, but he was also a scientist capable of clear, incisive observations over a wide range of scientific and cultural fields.

PART III

The Second Voyage

CHAPTER NINE

ONE YEAR ASHORE

CAPTAIN COOK could now enjoy a period of rest and relaxation with his family and friends. The Admiralty gave him command of another ship, HMS *Scorpion*, in order to keep him at full pay, but there is no evidence that the lords intended this to be more than a "holding" command. Already they had greater things in mind for James Cook.

The hardy *Endeavor* was refitted once more, given a new crew, and was sent off to the Falkland Islands as a storeship. In the morass of paper work collected by the Admiralty in ensuing years, it is impossible to trace what became of the *Endeavor* throughout the rest of her useful life. This is unfortunate, for, of all the famous ships of discovery, the collier of Cook's first voyage is probably the best described and was probably the best performer of all of Cook's ships—certainly she was his sentimental favorite.

In December, Cook and his family decided to visit the home of his youth in Yorkshire. Cook's father was now seventy-eight and comfortably settled in a small cottage near Great Ayton, but his mother had died a few years before. For Cook, resplendent in his new uniform, it was a triumphant return. The weather was the only thing that marred this sentimental journey. Winter had set in, and Elizabeth Cook was a poor traveler. Reluctantly, the explorer, who had been indifferent to cold and discomfort at sea all of his adult life, canceled the remainder of his trip in deference to his wife's wishes. Cook did, however, rent a horse, and he rode by himself to Whitby, where he was warmly received by that seafaring community and the men who had built the *Endeavor*.

Meanwhile, the Admiralty was busily planning a second exploratory probe into the South Pacific. As successful as Cook's voyage had been, there were still questions to be answered. The admirals and statesmen continued to be deeply concerned with the great unknown continent. There was little doubt that the country that first discovered it and first gained claim to its commerce would become the dominant sea power of Europe. In the *Endeavor*, Cook had pushed back a great part of the unknown continent's northern boundary, but there were still areas where it might exist. The French and Spanish were hot on the scent, and Alexander Dalrymple urged the Admiralty to make another effort to find "his" continent. King George gave prompt approval and this time the Admiralty had little difficulty in deciding on a voyage commander. Who else but James Cook had the stature and versatility to pursue this venture to a successful conclusion?

As for Cook, he was delighted. Moreover, he was consulted frequently for advice on the route to be taken, the ships, the crews, and the equipment.

Heeding Cook's advice, the Admiralty agreed that there would be more safety in numbers; consequently, two ships were purchased for the next expedition.

Again they were Whitby colliers. They were first named the *Drake* and *Raleigh*, but these names were changed lest they offend the Spanish, who had bitter memories of the exploits of those two British commanders. King George approved the names *Resolution* and *Adventure* as being more appropriate. At 462 tons, the *Resolution* was nearly 100 tons larger than the *Endeavor*. The *Adventure* displaced 336 tons. Both ships were less than two years old and they had been soundly built.

At this point Joseph Banks reentered the picture. He volunteered for the voyage, persuading the Earl of Sandwich to make a series of alterations on the *Resolution* to better accommodate his retinue of scientists. In this comic opera of bad decisions, which eventually turned the *Resolution* into an ungainly, top-heavy ship that could not even sail with safety down the Thames River, Captain Cook wisely held his tongue. Banks not only was his friend but also had the friendship and support of the Earl of Sandwich, First Lord of the Admiralty. Sir Hugh Palliser, Cook's old friend, now comptroller of the Navy, finally exploded in righteous seaman's indignation, and insisted that the alterations should be undone and that the collier be restored to original seaworthy condition. Moreover, he said that Captain Cook should supervise the work. Thus Joseph Banks withdrew from the expedition, having caused £5,000 to be spent in the senseless rebuilding of the ship. Instead of cruising the South Pacific, he charted an East Indiaman merchant ship and took his party on a "scientific" voyage to Iceland. Despite this whole foolish incident, Banks remained Cook's friend. This in itself speaks well for Captain Cook's tact and forbearance. By keeping quiet (probably knowing fairly well what the eventual outcome would be) Cook let the lubberly proceedings go on until they fell by their own weight. In that way, he was absolved of all blame; he did not arouse the ire of his patron Sandwich, nor did he lose the esteem and friendship of Banks.

Quietly, Captain Cook went about the business of preparation, and it must be said that the Earl of Sandwich spared no expense. This in itself was unusual in a naval administration noted for shortcuts, shortchanging, improper construction, and the misappropriation of official funds. When all was finished, Cook felt that the *Resolution* was "the properest ship for the service she is intended for, of any I ever saw."

The Admiralty's instructions for this voyage were made in close consultation with Cook. As a matter of fact, the explorer was asked to submit a plan which would settle once and for all the question of a southern continent. The agreed-upon solution was as brilliant as it was practical. Cook proposed to circumnavigate the world in high southern latitudes. By sailing east in the Antarctic summer, he could take advantage of prevailing westerly winds in a reasonable climate. When winter set in he could move north to a proven base of supply, such as Tahiti, make necessary repairs, revictual, and depart on an exploratory probe in the tropic island belts of the mid-Pacific. There he could take advantage of the easterly trades. Each year he would repeat the process, moving farther east along the ice edge in the "favorable" weather of Antarctic summer. Should he discover the famed southern continent, he would make the usual investigations and surveys and take formal possession of his discoveries for England. The latter intruction applied as well to any island that he might inspect during his tropical search.

By now James Cook's reputation drew seamen like a magnet. Selecting them was almost embarrassing. He picked his men with care and then had to ask the Admiralty for instructions with regard to the superfluous volunteers who still clamored to be taken. While the name Cook was a persuasive agent to recruitment, these London sailors were also attracted by the lure of the South Pacific and wondrous tales of amorous dusky maidens. To some extent, even in the twentieth century, this South Sea lure still draws men to the sea in ships.

Aboard the *Resolution* there were thirteen seamen and three officers from the former crew of the *Endeavor*. Lieutenant Clerke, who sailed with Cook on all three great voyages and who succeeded to command after his leader's death on the third trip, had been commissioned on Cook's recommendation when the *Endeavor* returned to England. So were the two other officers from the *Endeavor*, Pickersgill and Edgcumbe. In general, all of the seamen and officers were a happy choice. The *Adventure* was captained by Tobias Furneaux, who had sailed around the world with Wallis on the *Dolphin*. Furneaux was an experienced and competent captain, but he was not a second Cook—he did not have the same intelligence, energy, or determination. For example, when the two ships became separated in southern fogs, Furneaux returned to New Zealand and prepared to winter over ashore. When Cook arrived he directed Furneaux to get his ship ready for sea without delay, to accompany the *Resolution* on her tropic island search. Furneaux had the skills and competence of a good officer and seaman, but apparently had little perception or originality.

The withdrawal of Joseph Banks left a scientific vacancy that had to be filled. Here the Admiralty made an unfortunate selection. They engaged John Reinhold Forster, a German naturalist, and his son. These two, particularly the elder Forster, were quarrelsome companions, poor sailors, and miserable shipmates. Nevertheless, scientists were held in such esteem at the time that the Forsters were paid £4,000 for their services— almost as much as the purchase price of the *Resolution* itself, and a great deal more than Cook himself was paid. Two other expert assistants, Wales and Bayley, were engaged as astronomers, and proved to be much more acceptable shipmates. Each made significant contributions to the voyage, and afterward, both became successful educators. Wales sailed on the *Resolution* and Bayley was assigned to the *Adventure*. One more supercargo was added to the *Resolution;* this was William Hodges, an artist, who brought the total number of "gentlemen" aboard the flagship to a modest four. At the Cape of Good Hope, John Forster persuaded Cook to bring aboard a Swedish botanist, Anders Sparrman, as an additional member of the scientific team. Forster paid Sparrman £400 as a retainer.

The board of longitude sent four chronometers on the voyage. Three of them, made by a watchmaker named John Arnold, proved practically useless. But a duplicate of John Harrison's exquisite prize-winning instrument was carefully fashioned by a young craftsman named Larcum Kendall. This one was placed aboard the *Resolution*, where it kept excellent time. It is now in the Maritime Museum at Greenwich, England, where it is still running.

On July 13, 1772, one year to the day of the *Endeavor*'s return from her first voyage, Cook sailed from Plymouth. He followed a familiar pattern, stopping first at Madeira for wine and his inevitable onions. Shortly thereafter, he touched at Porto Praya on the island of St. Jago where he picked up fresh fruit, pigs, goats, and chickens. From there the two ships proceeded uneventfully to Cape Town, arriving on October 30. While his crews enjoyed a period of refreshment and shore leave, Cook visited the Governor and learned of two French expeditions in southern waters. These were Kerguelen and Marion, each with two ships. Kerguelen reported discovery of land at 48 degrees latitude, generally south of the island of Mauritius. Marion (Marc Marion du Fresne) was en route to Tahiti to return a young Tahitian who had accompanied Bougainville to Paris.

Before departing Cape Town, Captain Cook checked the antiscorbutic foods with care. Both ships carried sauerkraut, crushed oranges and lemons, malt, fresh wort, and portable broth. History has shown that portable broth had little beneficial effect, but at that time Cook was still experimenting. He felt certain that his preventive measures on the *Endeavor* were the solution to the prevention of scurvy, and he intended to demonstrate this forcefully and permanently on this cruise. At sea he insisted firmly that his other precautions be carried out. The crew's quarters were frequently washed, ventilated, and fumigated. In damp weather, areas below decks were dried with stoves—an unusual measure and an indication of the great care that Cook took of his men.

On November 22 the voyage south was resumed.

CHAPTER TEN

ANTARCTIC ICE EDGE, 1772-1773

FOR all practical purposes, James Cook began his famous second voyage of discovery at Cape Town, South Africa. It has been estimated that the *Resolution* sailed a total of seventy thousand miles during her three years away from England. The greater part of that distance was traveled in unknown waters, much of it along the edge of Antarctic ice. At first glance, the tracks of the *Resolution* seem to be a haphazard maze, crisscrossing with much abandon around the South Pacific. Admittedly, some of the routes do cross, either through design or at the whim of gale winds which frequently blew Cook's ship off course. However, there did exist a master plan for the voyage which Cook followed with dogged determination. The plan called for a west-east circumnavigation of the Antarctic during summer months. For such a voyage, three summers were required. The intervening winters saw the energetic Cook searching the tropical South Pacific, making enough surveys during these "rest" periods away from polar ice to justify the entire voyage.

After leaving Cape Town, Cook's immediate task was

to search south for the Cape of Circumcision, which had been discovered by a French explorer named Bovet in 1739. This rocky, desolate, icy island lies at latitude 54° 26' south, longitude 3° 24' east. Bovet's reported position was in error by over three degrees of longitude, which made it very difficult to locate. By sailing all around this mysterious point, even though he never sighted the island, Cook proved that it could not be part of a large continent.

As the history of polar exploration developed, mariners gradually realized that Europeans had one great misconception about the Antarctic. Geographers assumed that the climate in high southern latitudes would approximate that of similar latitudes in northern Europe. For example, latitude 54° north divides the British Isles in half, and is south of Norway and Sweden; it is even south of Moscow. Europe, however, is warmed by the Gulf Stream and its attendant weather, and therefore has a much milder climate. The west coast of North America is similarly warmed by the Japan Current. Students of American history will remember the motto, "Fifty-four forty or fight," as a proposed dividing line between Western Canada and the United States. But no warm current pushes far into the high latitudes of the Antarctic. The East Australian Current and the Brazil Current are both offshoots of the southern Equatorial Current, but neither runs very far south or has an equivalent influence on landmasses of the southern hemisphere. Consequently, the weather in high southern latitudes is much colder than in corresponding places of the northern hemisphere.

In Cook's time, however, the notion of a large continent in "temperate" latitudes above 40 degrees south persisted, so he went on with his search. Cook's main discovery in these waters was ice. The first mention of an "ice island" appears in the December 10 journal entry. On the next day the crew sighted an iceberg so large that everyone took it for land. As the ships continued south, the icebergs became more numerous. Pickersgill recorded seeing over forty in one day. Cook noted that some were two hundred feet high and over two miles in circumference. In spite of rigorous weather and frequent gales, he sailed through this ice-studded sea with scarcely a reference to its dangers. His journal is filled with remarks about birds, seals, penguins, the state of the weather, and scientific observations of different kinds of ice. On December 14 he lowered a boat for a conference with Captain Furneaux, and told the boat coxswain to bring aboard several pieces of ice when he returned to the *Resolution*. As he suspected, these pieces yielded fresh water. Thus assured of a plentiful supply of drinking water, Cook continued his southerly probe into the highest latitudes possible.

Despite gales and heavy seas, frequent snow, fog, icebergs and pack ice, the ships continued south. The decks were frozen and slippery, great icicles hung from the rigging, and it was bitter cold. Yet the general health of the men remained very good. On January 17, Cook crossed the Antarctic Circle and penetrated to latitude 67° 15′. This was the first time in the history of navigation that such a feat was accomplished.

In skirting the great field of pack ice, Cook found that he was working to the east, but was surprised to see the prevailing winds shift to easterly in extremely high latitudes. His grand plan called for a west to east circumnavigation, utilizing the westerly winds of the "roaring forties." Finding the pack ice impenetrable, however, he moved northeast once again to pick up favorable winds. At this time Cook did not know about the west wind drift, a steady current set up by the prevailing westerly winds. Nor did he know about the Antarctic convergence—a zone where cold north-flowing Antarctic waters meet less cold sub-Antarctic waters and sink below them. He noted abrupt changes in seawater temperatures as well as changes in marine life whenever he entered the convergence zone. Similarly, his inquiring mind led to the conclusion that there was a current setting to the northeast just off the ice edge. On one occasion in January the ships were blown to the west, and on returning east they found open water where a field of ice had existed four days earlier. Cook reasoned that such a large body of ice could not have melted in that short a time; therefore, it must have moved. Experts of the Antarctic are able to go back almost two hundred years to Cook's detailed observations, on which many of today's accepted explanations of Antarctic phenomena are founded.

The *Resolution* and the *Adventure* made a good team. For weeks they had sailed together in appalling weather, seldom losing sight of one another. In early February, however, they approached the fog that is common near the convergence zone. On the eighth they lost contact, and Cook sailed in circles for two days, firing guns and lighting flares of penguin fat in vain hopes of effecting a rendezvous. Cook then proceeded southeastward alone; he had given Furneaux instructions to cover situations like this. Furneaux searched for the *Resolution* for three days before deciding to seek winter quarters in New Zealand.

Sailing alone was nothing new to Captain Cook or to any of the former crew of the *Endeavor*, but it weighed heavily on John Forster and some of the new men. Cook took their minds off this problem with an investigation into a series of petty thefts which had occurred earlier. His journal merely notes that he punished "those in whose custody the stolen articles were found." The ship's log enumerates one dozen lashes each to William Brisco and Francis Taylor, and a half-dozen each to three others. Afterward Cook had his crew fall in at quarters while he inspected each man's hands. Those with dirty hands were punished by stopping their daily allowance of grog. By these actions the Captain gave the crew something else to discuss besides the disappearance of the *Adventure* and the desolate loneliness surrounding them.

For five more weeks the *Resolution* pushed eastward around the polar ice pack. With only one brief exception the weather was miserable. Cook sensed that he had pushed his luck far enough. "The time was approaching when these Seas were not to be navigated without enduring intense cold, which however by the by we were pretty well used to." Antarctic winter was approaching indeed. Cook had been in these waters for four months. He therefore concluded his first ice-edge cruise and stood northward toward New Zealand for a "short repose in a harbor where I can procure some refreshments for my people, which they begin to stand in need of. . . ."

The *Resolution* put into Dusky Bay, New Zealand, on March 26. She had been out of sight of land for one hundred and seventeen days. Only one man was sick. Cook anchored temporarily and sent out a fishing boat, which returned in a few hours with enough of a catch to feed the entire crew. The Captain then took one boat, put Lieutenant Pickersgill in another, and set out to find a better anchorage. Pickersgill returned excited by his discovery, a snug harbor that abounded in fish, timber, and fresh water. Cook promptly named it Pickersgill Harbor and moved the *Resolution* there. They pulled the *Resolution* into a small creek and moored her bow and stern to large trees, so close to the shore that branches intertwined with the ship's masts. One hundred yards from the stern there was a stream of fresh water. In this harbor the men of the *Resolution* rested for six weeks. They brewed spruce beer, hunted and fished, and ate until their jackets grew tight around their stomachs. Although they took precautions not to be surprised by the Maoris, the men saw very few natives.

Departing this happy hunting ground and snug harbor on May 6, Cook wrote an excellent set of sailing directions for posterity. He proceeded north through an inlet which proved that Dusky Bay was really not a bay but a sound—it is known as Dusky Sound today. In Queen Charlotte Sound the *Resolution* rendezvoused with the *Adventure* on May 18, to the general joy of all hands.

In conference with Furneaux, Cook learned that the *Adventure* had touched and then coasted the eastern shore of Tasmania while en route to Queen Charlotte Sound. Near the northeast tip, Furneaux met with bad weather, which drove him over toward New Zealand. He did not return to Tasmania, but on the basis of his short visit he assured Cook that the island was an integral part of Australia—a wrong conclusion, but one that Captain Cook accepted. Accordingly, Cook gave up his former plan of examining Tasmania as a winter project and determined instead to cruise eastward. Captain Furneaux was well bedded down to pass the winter in New Zealand, but Captain Cook was not ready to rest, and did not wish to "idle away the whole winter in port." He directed Furneaux to get his ship ready for sea and gave him written instructions to follow in case the ships became separated again. While Captain Furneaux was readying the *Adventure* for the next voyage, Cook took charge of the men on the *Adventure*'s sick list and cured them of illness with a diet of scurvy grass and antiscorbutics. On June 7 both ships were ready for sea.

CHAPTER ELEVEN

ISLAND-HOPPING, 1773

IN studying the South Pacific and the many explorers' tracks across it, Cook had noted a wedge-shaped section, south of the Tuomotus Archipelago, that was unexplored. This area was bounded on the east and west by the *Endeavor*'s track of 1769. It intrigued Captain Cook, who knew that it had to be probed for the southern continent; otherwise the geographers of London would never be satisfied—and neither would he. Accordingly, he decided to sail east from New Zealand between the latitudes of 41 and 46 degrees to longitude 135° west, and then north to Tahiti for rest and refreshment. In this manner he would pass well to the south of the *Endeavor*'s track and also bisect that wedge of unexplored ocean which bothered him. From Tahiti he could continue his westward island search and return to New Zealand for a short respite before setting out for the Antarctic once again.

For six weeks the ships plunged and rolled in the rough seas eastward of New Zealand. Cook found nothing of interest and was able to record few positive accomplishments. Yet he did prove that it was feasible to sail those waters in winter months, and by the absence of land he was able to rule out the possibility of the

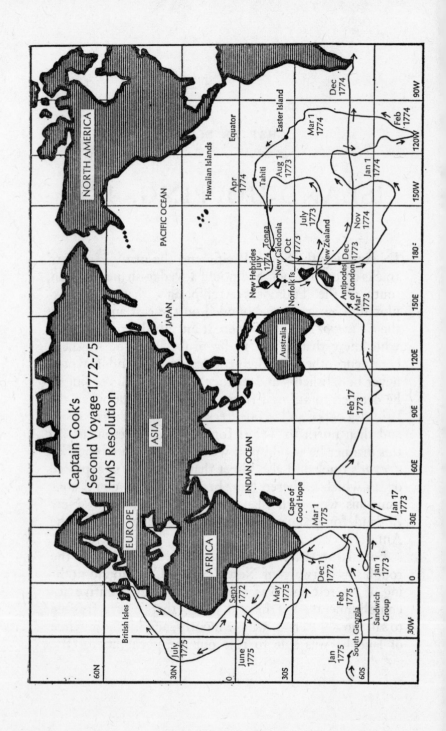

Captain Cook's
Second Voyage 1772-75
HMS Resolution

southern continent. Once again he had rolled back the northern extremity of Terra Australis Incognita. Reflecting on this fact, he wrote, "As I have now in this and my former voyage crossed this ocean from 40° south and upwards it will hardly be denied but what I must have formed some judgement concerning the great object of my researches—the Southern Continent. Circumstances seem to point out to us that there is none, but this is too important a point to be left to conjector, facts must determine it and these can only be had by visiting the remaining unexplored parts of this sea which will be the work of the remaining part of this voyage."

Cook's theory of ocean swells appears several times in his journals. The long hollow ocean swell, he reasoned, which continued in strength even after the wind which had set it in motion had disappeared, "plainly showed that we were never in the neighborhood of any large island." The great ocean swells of the South Pacific, which travel hundreds of miles without any interference by landmasses, are indeed positive indications of wide ocean expanse.

The six weeks' experience showed up differences in the incidence of scurvy on the two ships. By late July, twenty men were down with scurvy on the *Adventure*, and one had died. Health aboard the *Resolution* was good. Cook lowered a boat and sent over a ship's cook to the *Adventure*, with orders to feed Furneaux's crew a proper antiscorbutic diet. In order to alleviate the suffering of the scurvy victims, he made all possible speed north to Tahiti. In doing so he almost wrecked the *Resolution* on a coral reef south of the island.

As the ships approached Tahiti on July 16, Cook turned in at midnight, leaving instructions to lie to until

4 A.M. and then make sail for land. When he awoke at daybreak he found that his recommended course had not been followed and that both ships were dangerously close to the offshore reef. He gave immediate orders to haul off but at this moment the wind died. The tidal current swept both ships toward the reef, in spite of efforts by men in the ships' boats to hold off. Cook and Furneaux let go their anchors. The *Adventure*'s anchor held at the last moment, but the *Resolution*'s did not catch on the bottom in time. When it did, the ship's head swung around and her stern banged into the reef. By carrying out the kedge and coasting anchors and hauling away on connecting eight-inch hawsers, the *Resolution*'s crew slowly pulled their ship a few yards away from the coral. Later, the tide changed and a slight land breeze came up. Both ships cleared all danger by nightfall.

From the botanist Sparrman's journal there is an interesting sidelight on Captain Cook's character and his reaction in an emergency. Sparrman noted with relief the "lack of confusion with which each command was executed to save the ship." But he rather primly added, "I should have preferred however, to hear fewer 'Goddamns' from the officers and particularly the Captain, who, while danger lasted, stamped about the deck and grew hoarse with shouting." After the incident was over, Sparrman went down into the wardroom with the Captain and noted that while Cook had "from beginning to end of the incident appeared perfectly alert and able," he was now suffering "greatly from his stomach" and was "in a great sweat." He recovered quickly after a good dose of brandy.

Cook's first reception at Tahiti was not the joyous

one he expected. Many of his former friends had died or had fallen to an unimportant place in society. The first visitors aboard the *Resolution* were so open in their thieving that Cook threw them off his ship in exasperation. He even fired two musket balls over the head of his cabin guest, who departed in haste with several silver spoons from the wardroom. The natives ashore armed themselves with sticks and stones and gathered on the beach in a hostile mood. Cook ordered a four-pounder fired "along the coast." Astronomer Bayley was walking along the beach at this time, happily stretching his legs, when the four-pounder shot whistled by. The terrified natives took to the hills, while the frightened Bayley hastened back to the ship. In a few hours all was serene, and Cook's welcome thereafter was much more satisfactory, particularly when he moved to his old anchorage, Matavia Bay, on the northern side of the island.

During the seventeen-day visit at Tahiti, Cook was able to get only twenty-five pigs and one chicken from the natives. However, there were plenty of fruit, yams, and coconuts, as well as visits, dancing, and exchange entertainment, but altogether the stay left something to be desired. Cook continued his policy of treating natives with courteous civility and punishing his own men when their conduct was improper. On July 30, several marines and one seaman created a riot ashore from "making too free with the women." Cook put the culprits in irons that night and punished them with eighteen lashes the next morning.

At Huahine and other small islands the ships were received with more elaborate welcomes. Cook was entertained with great ceremony and exchanges of presents, and his old friends wept tears of affection to see him again. Trading was so brisk that when the ships departed the island chain they were loaded to the gunwales with four hundred hogs, several fowl, and great supplies of fresh fruit. Two natives joined the expedition: one named Odidde, aboard the *Resolution*, and another called Omai, aboard the *Adventure*.

Lieutenant Clerke's journal entry on September 17, the day of departure, gives a clear picture of the English sailor's love for "these happy isles." Noting that he left with reluctance, and that he had spent many happy days there in 1769 and 1773, Clerke gave these reasons: "You live upon, and abound in, the very best of Pork and the sweetest and most salutory vegetables; in the next place, the women in general are very handsome and very kind, and the men civil, and to the last degree benevolent . . . in short, in my opinion, they [the islands] are as pleasant and Happy spots as this world contains."

Sailing southwest in pleasant weather, Cook discovered several small, low wooded islands, which he named after Captain Hervey, one of the lords of the Admiralty. This small chain is now known as Cook Islands. Having no time to lose, he did not attempt a landing, but continued on toward Tongatabu, which had been discovered and reported by Tasman in 1643. These Friendly Islands (as he later named them) consisted of several groups of islets surrounding two larger islands. Tasman had named them Amsterdam Island (Tongatabu) and Middleburg Island (Bua).

These fertile and beautiful spots were inhabited by the most pleasant, friendly natives of the South Pacific. They were as great thieves as any elsewhere, but they confined their thieving to the shore "marketplace" or aboard the two English ships. The Tongans were big people with light brown skin and black hair. They laughed easily, wore very little clothing, and were completely trusting and unafraid. Their language was similar to that of the Society Islands but it was harsher; neither Omai nor Odidde could understand or translate Tonganese. Cook was very favorably impressed with the natives' energy and skill as farmers. He noted that their neat, carefully cultivated plantations produced such an abundance of food that "no one wants the necessaries of life, joy and contentment is painted in every face." Leaving wheat, peas, beans, and other seeds to add to the local produce, Cook reluctantly sailed on October 8. Southern summer was approaching, and it was time to think of another ice cruise in the Antarctic.

Nature gave the ships a preview of weather that might be expected during the next plunge south. The course from Tongatabu to Queen Charlotte Sound lay near the east coast of New Zealand's North Island. Cook had planned to return to Ship Cove for a brief refit, but a prolonged violent gale swept down on the two ships. Both were driven south of the entrance to Cook Strait, and they became separated again. Nevertheless, Cook brought the *Resolution* back and anchored in Ship Cove on November 3. The *Adventure* was not there, as he had hoped she might be, and although he waited three weeks, he never saw her again.

Cook was determined not to lose the season, so he left Queen Charlotte Sound on the twenty-fifth, having left written instructions for Furneaux in a wax-sealed bottle buried near a well-marked tree. Unfortunately he did not emphasize precautions against riot or surprise attack; if he had, it might have averted the massacre of ten men from the *Adventure* who were killed and eaten by the Maoris a few weeks after Cook sailed.

As a matter of fact, if he had only described an incident which convinced him beyond doubt of Maori cannibalism, it might have sounded sufficient alarm to Furneaux. The incident occurred aboard the *Resolution* two days before she sailed. Some of the officers purchased the head of a youth whom the Maoris had recently killed and brought it aboard ship. Lieutenant Clerke then asked a Maori who had accompanied him if he would eat a piece of flesh from the head, and "he very cheerfully gave his assent." Clerke described this in his journal as follows, "I then cut a piece and carried it to the fire by his desire and gave it a little broil upon the gridiron then deliver'd it to him—he not only eat it but devoured it most ravenously, and sucked his fingers ½ dozen times over in raptures: the Captain was at this time absent, he soon after came on board, when I cut and dressed my friend the other steak which he eat upon the quarterdeck before Capt. Cook and both were before the Ship's Crew."

Cook was outraged with horror, but considered that "any resentment I could show would avail but little." Some of the sailors vomited over the side. Captain Cook's scientific mind sought out an explanation. "Few considers," he wrote, "what a savage man is in his original state. . . . This custom of eating their enemies slain in battle (for I firmly believe they eat the flesh of no others) has undoubtedly been handed down to them from the earliest times." At any rate he now had an answer to the skeptics at home who always asked, "Have you ever seen, with your own eyes, a cannibal eat human flesh?"

The *Adventure* arrived four days after the *Resolution* had sailed. Captain Furneaux found the buried instructions and made haste to refit his ship for another extended cruise. On December 17 he sent a boat to "grass cove" for a supply of scurvy grass. When the men failed to return at night he became concerned, and sent Lieutenant Burney in the launch with a well-armed search party. Along the shore they found shoes, entrails, and a few hands—that was all that remained of the ten men, who, as Burney described, "were our very best seamen—the stoutest and most healthy people in the ship."

This loss occurred at a time when Furneaux received more bad news. All of his bread had gone bad, and the general state of his entire stock of provisions was not good. Cook's instructions were somewhat vague, so Furneaux concluded that he was on his own. Consequently he set out once more for the South Pacific alone. To his credit it should be noted that he cruised the ice edge until prudence warned him to call a halt to the voyage. He therefore made for the Cape of Good Hope, passing well south of Cape Horn, and sighted the southern coast of Africa on March 17. In doing so, he became the first man to circumnavigate the earth from west to east. The *Adventure* proceeded on to England, arriving a year before the *Resolution*. In retrospect, no one blames Furneaux for his actions. His ship had suffered considerable damage in the gale off New Zealand, but he used her to advantage during the long trek home.

CHAPTER TWELVE

SECOND ANTARCTIC PROBE, 1773-1774

COOK took the *Resolution* through Cook Strait and north to Cape Palliser, vainly hoping to sight the *Adventure*. He stayed in close to shore, sailing "from point to point" and firing guns every half hour. After two days of unsuccessful searching, Cook and his officers were of the unanimous opinion that the *Adventure* was not stranded on the New Zealand coast, and that no more precious time should be spent in this unprofitable pursuit. "I am under no apprehensions for the safety of the *Adventure*," Cook wrote, "nor can I even guess which way she is gone . . . I can only suppose that Captain Furneaux was tired with beating against the NW winds and had taken a resolution to make the best of his way to the Cape of Good Hope, be this as it may I have no expectation of joining him any more."

Taking departure from Cape Palliser on November 26, Cook noted with satisfaction that his crew was not dejected or worried about sailing alone. Course was set south southeast, and once again the *Resolution* headed for the lonely Antarctic seas. On December 7 navigators Cook and Wales reckoned that the ship's position was at the antipode of London. They were as far from home as they could possibly be. Astronomer Wales noted the event in his journal: "Between 7 and 8 o'clock, passed directly opposite to London and drank to our friends on that side of the Globe."

It is difficult to determine Cook's exact plans for his second ice cruise. The note for Furneaux, buried near a tree back in New Zealand, gave no rendezvous or orders. It merely stated that the *Resolution* would search "south and eastward" during the summer season, and that the ship would probably be at Easter Island or Tahiti near the end of March. All of this "will depend . . . upon circumstances." Later, when the *Resolution* was near the polar ice pack, Cook recorded more uncertain plans in his journal, saying "I intend to employ the whole of the ensuing season [there] and if I do not find a continent or isle between this and Cape Horn in which we can winter perhaps I may spend the winter within the Tropicks or else proceed round Cape Horn to the Falkland Islands. . . ." While all of Cook's records indicate a growing skepticism about the existence of a southern continent, it is interesting to see that his plans always allowed for its possible discovery. Captain Cook reasoned that there were enough theories about this mysterious land, so he sought facts.

As week after week rolled by, the *Resolution* piled up more statistical evidence of the continent's nonexistence. Dipping south toward the Antarctic Circle in December, the ship made good progress in spite of icebergs, logging 146 miles on December 14 and 116 miles on December 15. Here they encountered a large field of ice, bad weather, and fog. Cook shifted to the east and then north, barely managing to escape. Back in reasonably clear water and nothing daunted, he headed southeast again, crossing the Antarctic Circle (66½ degrees south) at longitude 143 degrees west on December 21. He remained below the Antarctic Circle for three days, moving east before a gale wind, in constant hazard from icebergs. A blizzard set upon the ship and once more the rigging became a mass of glittering icicles. On Christmas Day, Cook turned north, and held a traditional celebration in spite of the situation.

Forster wrote: ". . . the wind died away to a perfect calm . . . This being Christmas Day, the captain according to custom invited the officers and mates to dinner, and one of the lieutenants entertained the petty officers. The sailors feasted on a double portion of pudding, regaling themselves with the brandy of their allowance, which they had saved for this occasion some months beforehand, being solicitous to get very drunk, though they are commonly solicitous about nothing else." It must have been a successful celebration; Sparrman noted that "Sailors and marines . . . joked about the voyage, and vowed that, if they were wrecked on any of the 168 masses of ice surrounding us, they would certainly die happy and content, with some rescued keg of brandy in their arms."

By the twenty-sixth, over two hundred icebergs surrounded the ship, but the weather was clear and there was constant daylight, so the *Resolution* kept clear of danger. Cook headed north for a temporary relief from dangerous navigation, as well as a little sun and sleep before plunging south again. This permitted coverage of another area of the unexplored Pacific which bothered him. He was so far to the south of his easterly run from New Zealand in 1773 that about twenty degrees of longitude separated the two tracks. His brief northerly diversion probed this expanse, thereby eliminating another possible location of the southern continent.

When the *Resolution* started south again, Midshipman Elliott wrote with chagrin, ". . . We had all taken it into our heads that we were going straight for Cape Horn on our route home . . . and many hints were thrown out to Captn Cook, to this effect, but he only smiled and said nothing, for he was close and secret in his intentions at all times, that not even his first Lieutenant knew, when we left a place, where we should go next." Perhaps it is well that the officers and men did not know Captain Cook's intentions. This time he took the *Resolution* to latitude 71° 10′ south. Since that day no one else has ever taken a ship that far south in that longitude. He was only one hundred and twenty miles from Marie Byrd Land, which was discovered and named in 1929 when Admiral Byrd flew over it.

Cook was stopped by an immense field of ice which he fortunately saw just before fog set in. Retracing his steps, the Captain made one of the few entries in his journal which reveal his strong ambition: "I will not say," he wrote, "that it was impossible anywhere to get in among this ice, but I will assert that the bare attempting of it would be a very dangerous enterprise and what I believe that no man in my situation would have thought of. I whose ambition leads me not only farther than any other man has been before me, but as far as I think it possible for man to go, was not sorry at meeting with this interruption, as it in some measure relieved us from the dangers and hardships, inseparable with the Navigation of Southern Polar regions."

Cook and his officers came to the conclusion (later proven correct) that the ice extended "quite to the Pole or perhaps joins to some land, to which it had been fixed from the creation. . . ." The decision to turn back was sound, but where would they go? Only about a month of the season remained, time enough to reach Cape Horn but insufficient to complete the polar search or explore land if he found it.

Cook's decision is typical of him. It reflects his early philosophy, in 1773, when he said that he was not inclined to idle the winter away in port. The plan that he made for winter of 1774 was one of great design—a truly difficult undertaking, but one that intrigued his officers and made his men rejoice. Reasoning that he should not quit the "Southern Pacific Ocean with a good ship expressly sent out on discoveries, a healthy crew, and not in want either of stores or of provisions," he turned his attention to the islands of the Pacific. The tracks of the *Endeavor* and the *Resolution* ruled out the possibility of a southern continent, but Cook noted that there was "room for very large islands in places wholly unexamined: and many of those which were formerly discovered are but imperfectly explored, and their situation [location] as imperfectly known." He intended to sweep through these areas and raise the curtain of doubt and rumor which still hung over a large part of the ocean. His predecessors in these areas were hampered by more primitive methods of navigation, and were limited by the general health of their men. They could not fix positions as accurately as could Cook with his chronometer, nor could they spend sufficient time in exploration when their men were sick.

His first task would be to search for the land that Juan Fernandez was said to have discovered near latitude 38 degrees south; next he would look for Easter

Island. Afterward he planned to cross the Pacific from east to west on a route different from other navigators, fixing the position of any discoveries en route. If time remained, he would search for Quiros' Espiritu Santo and Bougainville's Great Cyclades before returning to Cape Horn in November. From there, he could prepare for and depart on a voyage into the South Atlantic, which would complete the exploration of the polar area.

Gradually the *Resolution* left the polar seas and bad weather in her wake. Soon the ice was gone and the warm tropic sun beat down on the ship's wooden decks. To everyone's surprise, himself included, the Captain became ill. He had worn himself out in the Antarctic, standing interminable watches and sleeping in snatches, often in wet clothing that he could not change for days at a time. He had an intestinal disorder (which he called a "billious colic") that was nearly fatal. He vomited constantly and could not eat anything.

His own journals do not show it, but those of other men aboard the *Resolution* reflect the great consternation and concern that pervaded the ship. Gunner's mate Marra wrote, "This day the Captain was taken ill, to the grief of all the ship's company." A few days later he noted that "The Captain this day much better, which might be read in the countenance of the other from the highest officer to the meanest boy on board the ship." Cook had been cured by a broth of fresh meat —John Forster's Tahitian dog, which he sacrificed without complaint. As a sign of his recovery, Cook wryly noted in his journal that he had "received nourishment and strength from food which would have made most people in Europe sick. . . ."

"The land of Juan Fernandez," supposedly discovered

in 1576, proved as nonexistent as the great southern continent. Cook was too weak to go up on deck, but he ordered a course for Easter Island. The second tropical sweep was about to begin.

CHAPTER THIRTEEN

NORTHWARD BREATHER, 1774

EASTER Island had been visited by the Dutchman Roggeveen in 1722, and by the Spanish in 1770, but its reported position was unreliable. The *Resolution* approached this barren, puzzling island on March 11, one hundred and three days since she had last seen land. It proved to be as inaccessible as it was poor. Cook never could find a decent anchorage, ending up after a three-day search in thirty-two fathoms of water one mile off the western shore. Weak as he was, Cook was the first ashore, meeting the natives in his habitual friendly way.

The natives proved to be friendly and unarmed, and some even wore European hats and handkerchiefs, which they had obtained from the Spanish visit four years earlier. The Easter Islanders appeared to be of a Polynesian type, speaking a language similar to Tahitian. In response to Cook's sign language for food, they gave the landing party some potatoes, plantains, and sugar-cane. In their dealings, the natives proved to be as expert thieves and as tricky as any that Cook had seen. They were constantly snatching at hats and rifling the Englishmen's pockets.

The place was interesting because of its strange statues, but it was a barren, unfertile land with little water. In less than two days Cook expressed his opinion of the island as follows: "No nation will ever contend for the honor of the discovery of Easter Island as there is hardly an Island in this sea which affords less refreshments and conveniences for shipping than it does, nature has hardly provided it with anything fit for man to eat or drink. . . ."

The great stone statues distributed about the island have remained a mystery to this day. They belonged to a culture that is unknown in the history of the Pacific. Some of the statues were prone and unfinished; others that were upright measured up to twenty-seven feet high and eight feet broad. The local natives did not worship these idols, nor did they know anything about them. Cook called the statues "monuments of antiquity" and marveled how a race that knew nothing about mechanical power could raise "such stupendous figures" and afterward place a cylindrical stone on their heads.

During the *Resolution*'s long voyage to Easter Island the menu had been salt beef and pork day after day. The ship's water supply was now poor and some of the crew began to show signs of scurvy. Cook decided to waste no more time, because he had "a long run to make" before he could find suitable water and fresh meat. His "long run" was for the Marquesas, a group of islands which had been discovered by Mendana in 1595 and never revisited thereafter.

After three weeks, sailing to the northwest of Easter Island, Cook found the beautiful mountainous islands of the Marquesas. He anchored in Mendana's harbor of Madre de Dios on the western side of the island of

Santa Christina. Here the trade winds funnel down a valley with great force, producing violent squalls at the bay's entrance. The gusty winds almost piled the *Resolution* on the rocky coast, but she slipped by with a few yards to spare. Immediately after the ship anchored, it was surrounded by canoes full of natives who were eager to trade and to steal.

The Marquesans were the finest physical specimens in the South Pacific. Lieutenant Clerke described them as "the most beautiful race of people I ever beheld." They were well proportioned, graceful, and fair-skinned. The crew of the *Resolution* were disappointed to see only a few women, but those that they did see were "very handsome and well made." Mitchel noted that they were "very shy, but however they was a little afterwards found to be women . . ."—a remark which testifies to the usual enterprise of a sailor ashore.

However well proportioned the Marquesans might have been, their livestock suffered by comparison. The pigs were so small that two sailors could devour one between them at a sitting. The crew struck up a brisk trade in fruit, pigs, fish, and coconuts, until "one of the young gentlemen ruined our market" by exchanging red feathers from Tongatabu for a pig. Thereafter, the Marquesans were not satisfied with anything else. When the bottom dropped out of the pig market, Captain Cook left in exasperation, having procured just enough fresh goods to stave off scurvy until he could reach Tahiti—the most reliable shopping port of his acquaintance.

In making for Tahiti, the *Resolution* threaded a dangerous passage through the "half-drowned islands" of the Tuamotu group. These atolls were so low that they were sighted with difficulty, frequently when the ship was too close for comfort. They had been discovered by Byron and Roggeveen, and were appropriately named "Isles of Disappointment." The natives were hostile and had nothing to trade. Cook paused long enough to determine the correct longitude and then pushed on for Tahiti, anchoring in Matavia Bay on April 22.

Cook was deliriously welcomed by a changed populace. Eight months before, the Tahitians had appeared morose and depressed, with little to trade and little inclination to be hospitable. Now they were happy, alert and eager. New homes and canoes were being built, plantations and gardens were well kept, and there was an abundance of pigs and other produce. Trade went on at a tremendous rate, but in spite of all of this prosperity and amiability, thieving flourished as before.

The *Resolution* was given a well-deserved rest and refit during the next four weeks. Cook's men caulked the sides, repaired sails, overhauled standing rigging, and landed empty water casks for refilling. Astronomer Wales landed his instruments, including the precious and reliable "Kendall watch." This chronometer had proven its worth to such an extent that Cook wrote that his primary reason for returning to Tahiti was to give Mr. Wales an opportunity to determine the chronometer's rate in a place of known longitude.

While this work was going on, Cook had an opportunity to observe maneuvers of the Tahitian war fleet, which was training for the conquest of a neighboring island. The invasion fleet was a brilliant gathering of between three hundred and four hundred double canoes, decked out with colorful flags and manned by almost

eight thousand fighting men. Cook watched an assault
exercise in which the canoes entered Matavia Bay from
the open sea, formed in a line abreast, and dashed full
speed upon the beach. Here the warriors leaped out,
picked up their war canoes, and carried them into con-
cealment among the trees. Within five minutes there
was no sign of the invading force. Cook was invited to
join forces in the forthcoming war, but he steadfastly
refused. He would have liked to stay to see the battle,
but the grand design of his tropic search spurred him on
once more.

The *Resolution* stopped at Huahine and also at
Raitea for short visits. Oree, the old chief at Huahine,
wept when Cook told him that he would return no
more, and urged him to "let your sons come, we will
treat them well." Throughout the history of these
islands, no explorer was ever on better terms with the
natives than Captain Cook. He exercised restraint, punished his own men for infractions of discipline, and
insisted on humane treatment and fair dealings. On one
occasion, when a native stole a musket from Cook's
sleeping sentry, the captain arranged for a joint public
punishment of both the thief and the sentry. The flog-
ging was carried out before hundreds of witnesses, who
offered no opposition to the unusual sight.

On his departure, Cook refused to take any natives
with him, for he did not want to incur an obligation
for their return. He was convinced that this would be
his last visit. He sailed June 4, taking his "final leave of
these happy isles and the good people in them."

He headed west toward Tonga, sighting en route
Lord Howe's Island, Palmerston Islands, and the Island
of Niue, which he called Savage Island, as a result of

an encounter with hostile natives. By June 27, Cook was able to anchor once more in the friendly islands of the Tonga group. This time it was at the island of Annamocka (which Tasman had named Rotterdam in 1643). The ship was well supplied with food in short order, but as friendly as the Tongans were, they continued to steal anything that they could carry off. In retaliation Cook seized two canoes for security and kept them until the stolen goods were returned. Shortly afterward, Cook was embarrassed when he was presented with a young woman as a gift. When he declined the offer, the girl's parents abused him unmercifully, so he beat a hasty retreat back to the ship.

From Tonga the *Resolution* sailed northwest, narrowly missing the Fiji Islands, but falling in with the New Hebrides on July 15. These were undoubtedly the same islands that Queirós had discovered and named Australia del Espiritu Santo. Both Bougainville and Carteret had passed through this group, but none had fixed any positions with Cook's accuracy. For a month and a half Cook sailed up and down the 350-mile island chain, "determining their situation." He stopped at Mallicollo, and at Tana where he rested for two weeks. He took a great number of astronomical observations and kept a running survey, mapping and exploring the entire area for posterity. It was a significant geographical achievement, but one that Cook cautioned was not as accurate as a geometrical plan like the charts that he had made during his five years off the coasts of Newfoundland.

Cook survived two incidents which nearly cost him his life. At Mallicollo a scuffle between a seaman and a native occurred on the quarterdeck of the *Resolution*. Cook rushed up on deck, where the native turned his drawn bow directly at him, giving the Captain no choice. He fired one barrel loaded with fine bird shot at the native. The man staggered, but turned the bow back on Cook. A second shot caused the startled native to drop the bow and jump overboard. Other natives began to shoot arrows at the crowded deck, so Cook ordered his gunner to fire a four-pounder into the air. This cleared the area about the ship, but a large band of four or five hundred warriors gathered at the beach, armed with bows and arrows, clubs and spears. Cook ordered a ship's boat and landed on the beach alone and unarmed, carrying a green branch as a sign of peace. It was a singular act of bravery and it was recognized as such by the primitive natives. An old chief handed his weapons to a compatriot, picked up a green branch, and met Cook at the water's edge. He took the big Englishman by the hand and led him into the crowd. Peace was restored.

At Eromanga, Cook displayed the inner sense and timing that served him so well on many an island shore. At this beach he was received with great courtesy and politeness. He was, he wrote, "charmed with their behavior," but he kept his eye "continually upon the chief and watched his looks as well as his actions." The chief made signs for Cook to haul his boat up on the beach. Suspecting that something was amiss, Cook stepped into the boat and gave orders to shove off. Immediately several natives attempted to hold the craft by force, and would not release it even when guns were pointed at them. "This made it absolutely necessary," he wrote, "for me to give orders to fire." The volley killed four men and dispersed the others. It narrowly averted a massacre.

It was now early August, and time to think of the

Antarctic again. Cook decided to return to Queen Charlotte Sound in New Zealand for last-minute preparations. He sailed southwest from Espiritu Santo and unwittingly made a new discovery. He found the island of New Caledonia, where men of the *Resolution* met, for the first time, South Sea natives who did not steal. The land resembled New South Wales (Australia), and while it was well watered and planted, it had no domestic animals. Cook presented the natives with a boar and a sow, and gave a pair of dogs to the chief. He remained at New Caledonia the better part of September, surveying the east coast. Time would not permit a longer stay, so Cook reluctantly departed, noting that it was the first time that he left a coast that he had discovered "before it was fully explored."

On October 10 he discovered Norfolk Island just south of New Caledonia. It was uninhabited, but the *Resolution*'s crew found a good supply of fish and cabbage palms. Cook's report on the vegetables and general abundance on the island led to its early settlement in 1788.

The timetable for the *Resolution*'s return voyage home was pressing. Cook proceeded south to Ship Cove, where he moored on October 9, and settled down for three weeks of preparation for the arduous trip ahead.

CHAPTER FOURTEEN

ICY VOYAGE HOME

AS soon as he landed, Cook searched for the bottle of instructions that he had left for Captain Furneaux. Finding it gone, and noting that a number of trees had been felled during his absence, he concluded that the *Adventure* had visited Ship Cove while the *Resolution* was on her tropic sweep. This relieved him of certain doubts and fears, but he was disturbed to learn from the natives that a landing party from "some ship" had been killed. Try as he did, he was unable to get a true story, and did not learn the facts about the massacre until much later, when he received a letter left for him by Captain Furneaux in Cape Town.

The inevitable diet of greens—celery and scurvy grass mixed with oatmeal and soup every morning, and peas and soup every evening—soon brought the *Resolution*'s crew back to glowing health. Fresh meat and fish furnished a welcome change from salted meat. Cook was particularly fond of Ship Cove as a place to refurbish his ship and strengthen his crew. He had taken particular pains to stock the surrounding country with fowl, pigs, and goats, and was pleased to see several of these animals running wild in the woods. He visited the ship's vegetable garden and was disappointed to find it almost overgrown with weeds due to its complete neglect by the natives, but he was pleased to see, nevertheless, that "many articles were in a flourishing state."

When he sailed on November 11, taking his departure from Cape Palliser for the third time, Captain Cook had some regrets. The Maoris of New Zealand did not have the warmth and hospitality of Tahitians, but he knew that he and his crew were welcome there. Three weeks before, when he had arrived at Ship Cove, the natives had hidden in the woods until they saw his familiar face. As soon as they recognized him and his party, Cook wrote, "they hurried out of the woods, embraced us over and over and skipped about like madmen." Cook's attitude toward the natives of the South Pacific, whether they were friendly Tongans or man-eating cannibals, was one of understanding and forbearance. Not many men of his time would make the following remark about the Maoris: "Notwithstanding they are *cannibals*, they are naturally of a good dispossion and have not a little share of humanity." He accorded to each race the dignity of mankind, and his simple methods worked. He always tried to land on their beaches as a friend, and it was his practice not to cut a tree or take a barrel of water without "first having obtained their consent."

Cook sailed south with all sails set, enjoying decent weather for the first time among the "roaring forties" latitudes. It was his first intention to cross the ocean in a mid-fifties latitude, but halfway across he decided that no land could be found in a higher latitude; so instead of working down to the polar ice edge, he steered directly for the western entrance of the Strait of Magellan. The trip across was uneventful, but it added more evidence against the possibility of a southern continent. When Cook sighted land near the tip of South America, he had, in his time, combed the South Pacific as thoroughly as one man could. All that remained for him to do was to complete his circumnavigation of the earth from Cape Horn to the Cape of Good Hope. If the continent did not lie in that one remaining expanse, it simply could not exist. Cook sensed that the end of his great work was approaching, and wrote, "I have now done with the Southern Pacific Ocean, and flatter myself that no one will think that I have left it unexplor'd, or that more could have been done in one voyage towards obtaining that end than has been done in this."

The *Resolution* was favored with good weather once again, so Cook took time out for his favorite hobby— surveying a strange coast. For two weeks he poked in and around the rugged coastline from Desolation Island on the west to Staten Island on the east. The charts that he prepared in that short time were not improved on for the next fifty-five years.

On arrival at Tierra del Fuego, Cook anchored on the western side and spent a few days replenishing the ship with wood and water. He sadly noted the loss of a marine, who, according to Cooper, "we imagine fell overboard last night as he was seen very much in liquor at 12 o'clock and was drowned." This brought the total ship's loss after two and a half years to four men—three by accident and one from a disease (not scurvy). The remaining men were as healthy and happy as when they set sail from Plymouth.

One reason that the *Resolution*'s crew was happy, no doubt, was the great interest that Cook and his officers had in their welfare. The Christmas season of 1774 provides a good example. On the twenty-fourth, Cook organized two shooting parties to find something fresh for Christmas dinner. He took charge of one party and Lieutenant Pickersgill led the other. They approached a large island from opposite directions, landing through the surf with great difficulty, and found a large flock of geese in molting season and unable to fly. They returned to the ship with sixty-two geese for the galley. In that desolate little harbor, the men stuffed themselves on goose and Madeira wine and forgot their troubles. Dour John Forster disapproved, and recorded the celebration as follows: "Our sailors well pleased to see their ship safe at anchor, had begun their holiday the evening before, and continued to carouse during two days without intermission, til Captain Cook ordered the greatest part of them to be packed into a boat, and put ashore, to recover from their drunkenness in the fresh air." Cook merely wrote the incident off with a casual, "our friends in England did not, perhaps, celebrate Christmas more cheerfully than we did."

Before departing Christmas Sound and Goose Island (as Cook named them), he spent some time with the natives of Patagonia. Remarking that they were an ugly, half-starved race whom he pitied, he noted that they were less than average height, once more dispelling earlier rumors that the Patagonians were giants.

Leaving Tierra del Fuego on January 3, Cook pushed southeast and crossed the South Atlantic between latitudes 55 and 60 degrees. The first land encountered was a desolate ice-capped island, which was sighted on January 14. Cook spent several days reconnoitering this forbidding area, landing and taking possession of South Georgia, the largest island of the group, which he named in honor of King George. Moving south to the pack ice at 60 degrees latitude, he sighted another group of islands, which he named Sandwich Land. Bad weather and ice fields kept him from sailing close enough to state positively that the southernmost isle was not part of a greater land area.

At this point Cook had formed a valid theory about icebergs, which led to his belief that a great continent did exist near the polar ice pack. At South Georgia he noted an "incredible" amount of snow and ice, which, he reasoned, increased in winter and broke off into floating islands in the spring and summer. He remarked, however, that South Georgia could not "produce the ten thousand part of what we have seen, either there must be more land or else ice is formed without it." These reflections, he continued, "led me to believe that the land we had seen the preceeding day might belong to an extensive tract and I still had hopes of discovering a continent."

From Sandwich Land, Cook pushed east in another search for Bovet's Cape Circumcision, which he had looked for in vain in 1772. Once more he failed to find it, passing some miles to the south in bad weather. By February 21 he had reached his earlier track of 1772, so he turned north for Cape Town, flattering himself that "the intention of the voyage has in every respect been fully answered, the Southern Hemisphere sufficiently explored and a final end put to the searching after a Southern Continent. . . ."

Arriving in Cape Town a month later, the *Resolution* remained there five weeks for necessary repairs. It was a pleasant occasion for Cook, who met and exchanged views with Captain Crozet, who had been Marion's second-in-command during the French visit to New Zealand in 1772. He bundled up copies of his charts and journals and forwarded them on to the Admiralty with Captain Newte, skipper of an English East Indiaman homeward bound from China. Botanist Sparrman left the ship, having completed his contract work with Forster. Three of the *Resolution*'s crew asked for their discharge papers, but they were replaced by four able-bodied seamen for the trip home.

It was not Cook's nature to make a hurried trip in a direct route to England. He stopped for food at St. Helena and for turtles on Ascension Isle. From there he veered west to the island of Fernando de Noronha, just to determine its exact longitude with the Kendall chronometer, which he now affectionately called "our trusty friend the watch." He repeated the procedure at the Azores, stopping at Fayal for water. On July 29, a little over three years since his departure from Plymouth, he arrived at Portsmouth.

Of his many achievements on this second voyage, he was, perhaps, proudest of his ability to keep his men alive and healthy. Only four men were lost in this tremendous trip through some of the most dangerous waters on the globe. He received a promotion to post captain, another interview with King George, and the accolades of educated society. For his victory over scurvy he was elected a fellow of the Royal Society and was awarded the Copley Gold Medal for his "admittance" paper on the disease.

Cook was temporarily given command of HMS *Kent*, but this was another "holding" command, to keep him on full pay. At his request he was appointed to the modest post of fourth captain of the Royal Hospital at

Greenwich. This gave him security that he had never had, for this institution was more of an old-sailors' home than a hospital. Senior officers appointed to direct the administration of Greenwich Hospital could live out their lives in comfortable buildings set among pleasant lawns that sloped to the banks of the Thames River. It was the "safe harbor" that many sailors dream about, but no one, including Cook, felt that Captain Cook had dropped anchor for the last time.

PART IV

The Third Voyage

CHAPTER FIFTEEN

NOAH'S ARK, 1776-1777

CAPTAIN COOK was now famous, and a coveted guest in the most fashionable London drawing rooms. The quiet sea captain, who seldom discussed his plans aboard ship, became an affable conversationalist. Ahead of him lay a distinguished career in comfortable retirement. He had plenty of work to do. There were charts to complete and consolidate into a master map of the South Pacific, and there were his journals. The published account of his first voyage, which had been prepared by a well-known London literary hack, had been poorly done. After a false start with the Forsters, Cook decided to write his own account of the second voyage. The Admiralty supported him wholeheartedly, and arranged for him to have the assistance of well-educated and respected Canon John Douglas.

James Cook did not regard his assignment to Greenwich Hospital as a passport to idleness. In the first place, when he had applied for the position he had carefully inserted the provision that he "would on no account be understood to withdraw from that line of service which their Lordships goodness has raised me to, knowing myself capable of ingaging on any duty which they may be pleased to commit to my charge." In other words, his finances dictated the necessity for full pay, which the post at Greenwich fulfilled, but he did not wish to be considered permanently on the shelf. As a matter of fact, Cook dreaded the prospect of continuous shore duty. In August, 1775, he wrote his old friend and former employer, John Walker, "My fate drives me from one extreme to another; a few months ago the whole southern hemisphere was hardly big enough for me, and now I am going to be confined within the limits of Greenwich Hospital, which are far too small for an active mind like mine."

Meanwhile, the Admiralty was busy repairing the *Resolution* for another voyage of discovery. The purpose of this trip was to look for the eighteenth-century will-of-the-wisp—a northwest passage between the Atlantic and Pacific oceans. Because of the difficulties with the American Colonies, trade routes for the British Empire were shifting from the Atlantic to the Indian Ocean and the Far East. Tea trade with China was all important, but it had to be conducted via the Cape of Good Hope, which was not only the longest British commercial shipping route but also the most vulnerable in time of war. A route across the tip of North America, if it could be found, would be much safer, shorter, and, on the whole, preferable. In over one hundred years of trading in Canada, English expeditions had proven the impossibility of a navigable channel leading to the Pacific from the south or western side of Hudson Bay. The eastern face of North America had been explored again and again, and many lives had been lost in unsuccessful attempts to locate a passage. However, no one had tried from the Pacific side, entering Baffin Bay or Hudson Bay from the north. So important was this passage at the time that a standing reward of £20,000 was offered for the first ship to effect a crossing through it.

A subsidiary reason for the voyage was the navy's obligation to return a Tahitian to his native land. Captain Furneaux had brought a native of Huahine, named Omai, back to England in 1774. During his visit to Great Britain, and later to France, Omai had enjoyed himself hugely and was somewhat of a celebrity. He was supported by the charities of England's noble families, who at length had become bored with the novelty of his sojourn. The time had come for his return to the South Pacific.

The lords of the Admiralty were reluctant to order or even to ask Captain Cook to undertake a third voyage. But they did ask for his advice and cleverly got around to the question of finding a man to lead the expedition. The bait was sufficient; Captain Cook promptly volunteered, asking only that the post at Greenwich, or something similar, be held for his return. Once more he began the familiar preparations for a long voyage.

The two ships this time were to be the *Resolution* and another, smaller Whitby collier of about three hundred tons, the *Discovery*. Fitting out once again at the royal dockyards of Deptford, the *Resolution* fell victim to the poor work and administrative malpractice which characterized Lord Sandwich's tenure as First Lord of the Admiralty. Caulking was poor, the rigging was substandard, and the spare sails fell early victims to rot and mildew. The ship leaked so badly that water poured into the crew's quarters from the upper decks. The *Resolution*'s poor material condition caused delays throughout the voyage, and indirectly led to Cook's death at Hawaii.

Many of Cook's officers were not new to him. His first lieutenant on the *Resolution* was Lieutenant Gore, who had sailed with him on the *Endeavor*. Charles Clerke, of both *Endeavor* and *Resolution* experience, was appointed captain of the *Discovery*. With him as first lieutenant was James Burney, a midshipman on the previous voyage, who was destined for a long, distinguished career as a naval officer and historian. There was also Bayley, the astronomer who had accompanied Furneaux, and a promising young midshipman, George Vancouver, who later led an important exploration of the northwest coast of North America.

Cook did not take an independent astronomer on the *Resolution* for this voyage, but he did take the chronometer that had proved invaluable on his previous trip. He and his assistant, Lieutenant King, were to be responsible for observations. His sailing master was also an excellent navigator who already had made a reputation for preparing exquisite, accurate charts. This was William Bligh, who, in his notable but irascible career, was deposed twice by mutiny, first on the *Bounty* and second as governor of New South Wales. Nevertheless, for the record it should be noted that Bligh was as resourceful and brave as he was pugnacious. This is evident from his record open-boat voyage after he had been cast off the *Bounty*, as well as his conduct in the Battle of Copenhagen, where Lord Nelson commended him for gallantry.

Of all the officers who served under Cook, the only failure was Lieutenant John Williamson. He was suspected of cowardice on the basis of his conduct at

Hawaii. Unfortunately it was not until he was promoted to captain that this trait was positively proven. Years after the Hawaiian incident he was court-martialed for cowardice as captain of the *Agincourt* in the Battle of Camperdown.

King George's consuming interest in farming and husbandry caused the two ships to become veritable menageries. The King wished to distribute seed and to populate the more promising South Sea islands with domestic animals. When Cook sailed he carried sheep, goats, pigs, chickens, cows, dogs, and horses. All they needed, he said, were "some females our own species" to resemble Noah's Ark. Now that he had learned to keep his men alive on long voyages, he had to find a similar solution for the forecastle barnyard. On previous voyages, he had carried some animals which were slaughtered for the ship's larder. They never lasted very long. However, here he faced at least a year of care and feeding his flock, a chore which necessitated many extra stops for fresh water and fodder. The ordinary seaman's reaction to the mooing, baaing, grunting, and stinking extra cargo is not difficult to imagine.

Through the extravagances of relatives, Captain Clerke suddenly found himself in debt and sought sanctuary from moneylenders in the "liberties of the fleet," a pestiferous prison where he contracted consumption. This necessitated separate departures. Cook sailed in July, 1776, on the anniversary of his departure four years earlier, which his crew viewed as a sign of good luck. Although Clerke was in the first stages of his illness, he managed to elude his creditors and sail with the *Discovery* on August 1. He joined the *Resolution* at Cape Town, where an impatient Cook was waiting. The voyage to South Africa had revealed many defects of the ship which had to be corrected. Finally ready, the two ships sailed at the end of November, heading south on a temporary diversion to find and examine recent French discoveries. The barren rocky islands seen by Marion and Crozet, as well as the discovery of desolate Kerguelen, were of no practical value, so Cook moved on toward New Zealand, stopping off at Tasmania for forage and trees to replace broken spars. If he had not been pressed for time, no doubt Cook would have coasted the shores of Tasmania and discovered its insular nature, but he pressed on, still accepting Furneaux's unsound theory that Tasmania was a part of the Australian mainland.

The ships arrived at Queen Charlotte Sound on February 12, where they rested for two weeks and prepared for a tropic cruise to dispose of their livestock and Tahitian passenger. The apprehensive Maoris thought that Cook had found out the truth of the *Adventure*'s massacre and had returned to exact vengeance. On the contrary, Cook recognized the incident as spontaneous and unpremeditated, and generously decided to let the matter drop. In doing so, he lost face with the natives, whose own sense of justice would have required bloodletting.

The cruise toward the tropic belt was slow, and the first islands sighted either were uninhabited or the natives were terrified of the animals and would have nothing to do with them. Unable to dispose of his menagerie, Cook procured fodder and water where he could and set a course for the Friendly Islands. They arrived at the island of Mango near the end of April and spent a leisurely two months with the friendly, fun-loving Tonganese. The animals were put ashore at Tongatabu to graze while the crews cleaned the ships and enjoyed a temporary freedom from farmers' chores. Cook filled his journal with acute observations of the customs and rituals of the Tonganese, thus unknowingly making significant contributions to later anthropological studies of South Sea Islanders. The Tonganese chiefs willingly accepted token presents of sheep, goats, and cattle, and vied with one another in developing new methods of stealing more. Once again Cook had to take retaliatory measures to obtain the return of the stolen animals.

Cook sailed with a respectable quota of animals for distribution in Tahiti and the outlying Society Islands. When he arrived in August his flock was in a surprisingly healthy condition, having been through the cold of the Antarctic and drought of the hot doldrums without ill effects. Fortunately Cook had kept two horses, and was able to impress the Tahitians sufficiently to make them forget earlier gifts from two Spanish ships. In full uniform, Captains Cook and Clerke took daily exercise on horseback, "to the astonishment of a great train of spectators."

The Tahitian visit followed its usual friendly course. Once again Cook was invited to assist the Tahitians at war with neighbors and again he refused. As he had done in Tongatabu, he concentrated on observations of native customs, culminating with attendance of celebrations over a human sacrifice. Chief Otoo granted Cook and his officers permission to observe the strange ceremony, which purported to obtain assistance from the gods in bringing the inter-island war to a conclusion. When Cook arrived the victim had already been slain, "having been privately knocked on the head with a

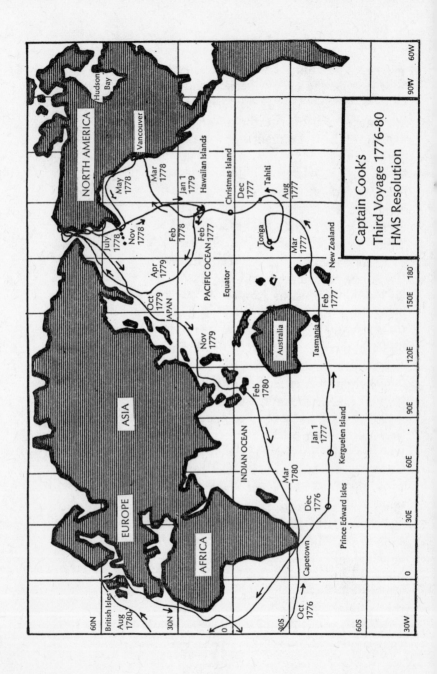

Captain Cook's
Third Voyage 1776-80
HMS Resolution

stone." Captain Cook was repulsed by this barbarous custom, but recorded it in great detail. Pointing out that he was not aware that the victim had committed any crime, Cook stated that these sacrifices were not uncommon, and that when any of the great chiefs thought that a sacrifice was necessary, he merely selected a victim and sent his servants to kill the unfortunate man. Cook and his officers remained silent during the ceremony, but after it was over they "made no scruple in giving out sentiments very freely upon it, and of course condemned it." Omai explained to the Tahitians that even the greatest man in England would be punished if he killed his servant. Chief Otoo did not appear greatly impressed with the British reaction to the ceremony, but the rank and file Tahitians listened to Omai with great interest.

Before leaving Tahiti, Cook took great delight in countering a bit of Spanish propaganda. In between his second and third voyages, the Spaniards had visited Tahiti and had erected a cross bearing the inscription, "Christus vincit. Carolus III imperat, 1774," as if Tahiti were their own discovery. On the other side of the cross Cook cut the words, "Georgius Tertius Rex, Annis 1767, 1769, 1773, 1774 et 1777," thus marking Wallis' discovery of the island and his own frequent visits.

At the end of September the two ships left Tahiti for a series of extended visits at neighboring islands. Cook landed Omai at his native Isle of Huahine, building a house and planting a garden for him. He equipped the house with the many gifts that had been showered upon the "noble savage" back in England. By native standards Omai was now a man of wealth and stature, but his vanity got the better of him and neither he nor his wealth long survived. The *Resolution*'s last stop was at Raiatea, where three of the crew tried to desert. With his usual firmness in cases like this, Cook seized native hostages to ensure delivery of the deserters.

A year and a half had elapsed since Cook had left Plymouth; he finally left the charms of the Society Islands on December 7, 1777, and headed north for the most important task of his voyage—the search for a northwest passage.

On Christmas Day he discovered near the equator a small low island which was uninhabited and had little value. He named it Christmas Island, and spent several days there fishing and hunting turtles. Before he left, he planted coconuts, melons, and yams in the questionable soil that was "light and black, evidently composed of decayed vegetables, the dung of birds and sand." With the exception of its use in the twentieth century as a strategic airstrip and location for nuclear tests, Christmas Island has remained "of little value."

As he sailed north in early January, 1778, he began to see tropic birds and turtles in increasing numbers. These signs of land brought an air of eager anticipation in both ships, and the crews realized that they were on a voyage of discovery once more. Early in the morning of January 18 the lookouts sighted islands of significant size and beauty. Since Cook was on a tight schedule to explore hundreds of miles of North American coast, he stopped at only two islands of the Hawaiian chain. He did, however, indicate in his journal that he considered the Sandwich Islands, as he called them, among his most important discoveries, which he fully intended to explore in detail at a later time.

Although his first visit to the Hawaiian Islands was necessarily short, Cook observed the land and people closely, noting the similarity between Hawaiian and Tahitian languages and customs. In appearance the natives of these islands resembled Tahitians and were as adept at and prone to thieving, although they traded honestly. The first native aboard the *Resolution* attempted to take the lead line used for soundings. He appeared surprised when he was restrained, saying, "I am only going to put it in my boat." Cook rapidly gained the impression that the natives viewed as fair game any movable item that they could carry from the ship. They were, incidentally, astonished at everything they saw, indicating without a doubt that they had never been on board a ship before.

Cook visited the island of Kauai to look for water, noting with surprise that he was greeted everywhere as a great chief. The natives invariably prostrated themselves when he approached and remained in that humble position until he had passed. In his lengthy description of the people and customs, Cook included this interesting observation: "They are an open, candid, active people and most expert swimmers we had met with; in which they are taught from their very birth: It was very common for women with infants at the breast to come off in canoes to look at the ships, and when the surf was so high that they could not land them in the canoe they used to leap overboard with the child in their arms and make their way ashore through a surf that looked dreadful."

Leaving some goats and pigs to breed on the island of Niihau, Cook reluctantly let his timetable for Arctic exploration take him away from his interesting discovery. He left on February 2, vowing to return. The *Resolution* and the *Discovery* now headed northeast for the American continent.

CHAPTER SIXTEEN

SEARCHING FOR THE NORTHWEST PASSAGE, 1778

SIR FRANCIS DRAKE was the first Englishman to set foot on the west coast of North America. In 1579 he beached the *Golden Hind* for repairs in an unknown harbor of California, sailing west from there to complete his famous voyage of circumnavigation. During the two hundred years following Drake's landing, Spaniards settled securely and permanently in California, but they seldom ventured far north of what is now San Francisco. A Greek pilot, known by the Spanish name of Juan de Fuca, did sail into the higher latitudes off the west coast and discovered the great strait which bears his name.

However, the greater part of the northwest coast was still not well-known by the eighteenth century. Bering, the Danish explorer sailing for Peter the Great of Russia, was the first to record a separation between the continents of Asia and North America. In 1728 he passed through the strait that separates the two land-masses and also sailed along the Aleutian chain. But the privations and hardships that he suffered caused his premature death before he could return and explore the area fully. Cook transited Bering Strait, determining the exact distance that separates the two continents and surveying the coasts on either side. In his Alaskan cruise, he found land where there had been only a geographer's conjecture. This was quite different from his second voyage in which he sailed all over Dalrymple's "southern continent" to prove that it was not there. His third voyage gave form and substance to a great unknown portion of North America. Most of Cook's biographers pay very little attention to this accomplishment and concentrate more on the beautiful islands and interesting people of the tropics. Nevertheless, for his work along the fog-bound, stormy coasts of Canada and Alaska, Cook ranks with the foremost explorers of America.

Cook's instructions required him to touch the west coast of North America at New Albion (as Drake named it), latitude 45 degrees north. From there he was to push north rapidly in search of the northwest passage. His exploration of this part of the world generally has not received the credit it deserves. Actually it equaled his exploration of the eastern coast of Australia. From the landfall south of the Strait of Juan de Fuca, somewhere on the coast of Oregon, Cook explored thirty-five hundred miles of uncharted North American coast, usually in fog and stormy weather. Many of the geographical names found in that area today had their origin in this voyage. It was a dangerous undertaking for a sailing ship, because most of the prevailing winds set toward the shore. However, Cook was perhaps the greatest "onshore" sailor who ever lived. Where many captains would have given this coastline a wide berth for safety, he sailed in closely, taking soundings, bearings, and celestial observations whenever weather permitted.

He sighted New Albion on March 7, and from there was pressed by his timetable to make a quick passage north. Bad weather and haste precluded a close examination and so he inadvertently missed the Strait of Juan de Fuca, and coasted the seaward side of Vancouver Island without discovering its insular character. It fell to midshipman George Vancouver to return years later for the detailed coastal survey that gave him geographical immortality.

At the end of March, Cook reached Nootka Sound (he named it King George Sound) in Vancouver Island, and remained there four weeks for repairs. The condition of the ships was disgraceful; the *Resolution*'s foremast had rotted at the base. Whole seams below the water line had lost all oakum and required complete caulking. Captain Cook could have called a halt to the voyage right then, and returned to England with complete justification, blaming his failure on the miserable work done by Deptford Yard. Fortunately there was an abundant supply of timber at Nootka Sound and there were competent carpenters aboard. Cook personally led a party of men into the woods to cut a tree for a mizzenmast.

The natives of Nootka Sound were eager to trade, offering fish, furs, carved work, and even human skulls and hands. In exchange they sought knives, nails, and pieces of iron or tin, but they shunned beads and cloth. These Indians were a swarthy, simple race, with black straight hair and painted faces. They were amiable and peaceful enough, but were so dirty and foul smelling as to discourage any great friendship or familiarity. None of the women, Cook thought, "had the least pretentions to being called beauties." They were small, had crooked legs, and little black eyes that were "devoid of sparkling fire."

He explored the villages, noting that there were no domestic animals or cultivated crops. He was particularly impressed with the climate, which was "infinitely milder than on the East Coast of America under the same parallel of latitude." In April the grass was already a foot long. The native houses were made of wood, stretching as much as one hundred and fifty feet in length and twenty-four to thirty feet in width, and were divided into a series of adjacent apartments. Cook was struck with the number of large images (totem poles) which were placed about the homes, and when some of his officers remarked that the statues were native gods, Cook disagreed. If they were, he said, "they held them very cheap, for with a small matters of iron or brass, I could have purchased all the gods in the place, for I did not see one that was not offered me. . . ."

At last, on April 26, the ships were ready and put out to sea, only to find strong signs of an approaching storm. For two days the wind blew at gale strength, drenching the ships with rain so heavy that the men could not see the length of the *Resolution*'s main deck. In order to avoid being blown on a lee shore, Cook steered southwest into deep water. After the storm passed, a fresh gale wind persisted from the southeast, so rather than wait for better weather to resume coastal exploration, Cook sailed north out of sight of land until May 1. There he sighted a mountain which he named Mount Edgecombe in honor of his former marine lieutenant. Two days later he sighted Mount Saint Elias. He was now in the Gulf of Alaska, where the coast tends west toward the Alaska Peninsula and the Aleutian Islands. Cook landed on Keyes Island May 11, leaving a bottle with an inscription to identify his visit.

The ships put into an inlet near Cape Hinchingbroke (named after the Earl of Sandwich's country estate), and had a brief encounter with natives. Several boarded the *Discovery* early one morning, "with a view to plunder, thinking they would find everybody asleep." The Indians drew their knives and motioned the officer on watch to keep clear. When the aroused crew poured from the forecastle with drawn sabers, the intruders quickly withdrew to their canoes, and began describing to the others how much longer the English knives were than theirs. Captain Cook gathered from this episode that the natives had never seen firearms before, and was pleased that he could leave the inlet without firing on them.

Once again *Resolution*'s carpenters went to work caulking seams around a bothersome leak. This time the ship was heeled on the beach to expose defective seams underneath the sheathing. During this sojourn a few natives paid friendly visits, making a disturbing appearance, however, with horizontal slits in their under-lips. A seaman remarked that one of them looked as if he had two mouths. Some of the women had their lips pierced instead of slit. They fixed small pieces of bone inside the lip, and held them in place with thread run through the pierced holes. This barbarous ornament was not only an impediment to speech but also gave the women the appearance of having a double row of teeth in the lower jaw. Otherwise, in general appearance and dress, natives of the Hinchingbroke area resembled the Esquimaux of Greenland.

With the ships patched up once more, Captains Cook and Clerke proceeded southwest along the shoreline until they reached a large inlet that stretched out among hills to the north. To rule out the possibility that this might be the beginning of a strait, Cook took the little expedition on a four-day search inland. When it was no longer safe for the ships to go any farther, Bligh continued the search with ship's boats. He returned at 2 A.M. on June 1 to report that the inlet turned into a freshwater river at its head. This killed all hopes of finding a passage here. Cook named the inlet for himself and took possession of the country and river in the name of the king, moving out promptly after the ceremony to continue his westerly coasting.

It was becoming evident to Cook that the continent extended much farther to the west than the latest charts showed. This made a northwest passage to Hudson Bay or Baffin Bay less probable, but he went on with the survey, investigating every inlet or sound that appeared promising.

At the end of June, the ships passed north of Kodiak Island, continued on to Unalaska, and then crossed through the Aleutian Islands, turning northeast. Cook then explored the northern side of the Alaska Peninsula, penetrating well into Bristol Bay. Here he noticed that the Indians appeared to have met Europeans before. Some came out in skin-covered canoes to deliver a letter to him. The messenger bowed politely and handed up a packet. No one on either ship could read the letter; it was written in the Cyrillic alphabet, presumably in Russian. Its contents and origin have remained a mystery to this day.

Surviving one grounding and several near-misses on jagged rocks, the two tireless ships continued northward. Cook followed the coast as well as he could, considering the weather and incessant fog. He reached the westernmost point of the continent on August 9, and named it Cape Prince of Wales. He was now just below the Arctic Circle in Bering Strait and the best part of the summer season was gone. Realizing that he would have to return the following summer to complete his mission, Cook decided to explore both sides of the strait and to work north as far as the ice and weather would permit. Then he would retire to find suitable quarter for the winter.

Cook landed on the Asian side of Bering Strait on August 10, undoubtedly the first man to ever set foot on every continent. Here he found natives somewhat like those on the American shores, but they were larger physically and more timid. Cook obtained enough salmon to feed his men but there was little else to be had on this desolate land. He crossed the strait again, touching the American shore, and worked north to an impenetrable wall of ice at latitude 70° 44′ north. The ice rose to a height of ten to twelve feet at the water's edge, with an extremely rugged surface. He spent several days cruising the ice edge, working back to the Asian shore, but it was impossible to penetrate farther. Walrus inhabited the pack ice in "prodigious number," and were both a source of food and an aid to navigation. In darkness or in fog, Cook sailed the ice edge "being partly directed by the roaring of the Sea Horses" (as he called them).

By August 29, even stubborn Captain Cook felt that it was time to turn back. His thoughts now turned to wood and water supplies, and how he could spend the winter "so as to make some improvement to geography and navigation." He resolved to search the American coast for a good harbor and water; if he failed to find them, he would anchor at Unalaska. The ships continued to work well together, taking soundings and bearings for transcription to chart after chart. They explored Norton Sound without finding water, so at length they steered for Samganooda Harbor (English Bay) in Unalaska, arriving there October 3.

Carpenters were put to work on the *Resolution*'s leaks while the men busied themselves finding berries (there were no vegetables) and fish. On October 8 an Indian appeared carrying a rye bread salmon pie as a gift for the two ship captains. Cook and Clerke assumed that the presents came from Russian traders, so in return they sent a few bottles of rum, wine, and porter which they "thought would be as acceptable as anything we had." A few days later they made contact with Russian sailors in the fur trade, as well as one Ismyloff, who was a world traveler and the most important Russian in the islands. Cook enjoyed the time spent with these men of the sea. While they could not converse, they shared a common interest in charts and navigational techniques. The Russians freely disclosed everything they knew about the area, offering charts for Cook's inspection. He gathered that aside from Bering's probes along the Aleutian chain, no other Russian expeditions had explored the Alaskan coast.

By the time the ships were ready for sea, Cook and Ismyloff had become warm friends. Captain Cook presented the Russian with a Hadley's octant and noted with satisfaction that his friend quickly learned how to use it. Ismyloff agreed to forward a letter and a chart to the British Admiralty for Cook, who expected to spend at least another year in the Arctic. The Russian was as good as his word; the letter took a year en route, but it was finally delivered after a long overland journey across Siberia and Europe.

The expedition sailed for Hawaii on October 26. Cook planned to spend the winter there and return to Kamchatka by the middle of May. He gave Clerke instructions to cover the possibility of separation en route, naming Hawaii as the first place of rendezvous and Petropavlovsk as the second. Ten days out of Unalaska, when the ships were in a calm, Captain Clerke came aboard the *Resolution* to inform Cook of a fatal accident on the *Discovery*. The main tack had given way several days earlier in a storm, killing one man and injuring three others.

With the approach of moderate weather, the ships moved south at a better pace, making a landfall at the island of Maui on November 26. The island was beautiful, and friendly natives came out in canoes by the hundreds, but there was no anchorage. Cook coasted Maui in an unsuccessful search, until he sighted the great slopes of Mauna Loa and Mauna Kea on the island of Hawaii. Time was running out for Captain Cook, but he had no idea that in steering for Hawaii, he had made a fateful decision.

CHAPTER SEVENTEEN

HAWAIIAN
HOSPITALITY, 1778-1779

AT first Hawaii was a maddening, frustrating experience. The island lay before the two ships in all its lush beauty, but there was no anchorage. The green hills sloped gently down to the water's edge and then dropped off in steep sheer cliffs that were dotted with clear waterfalls. The ships sailed along the eastern shore, frequently surrounded by canoes laden with "hogs and women," fruit and flowers. Trade was brisk enough to satisfy the sea-tired men and replenish their diet, but they needed a period of rest at anchor.

A storm separated the two ships on Christmas Eve, and they were unable to rejoin each other until January 6. The *Resolution* suffered serious damage to her rigging and for a while was in danger of shipwreck, but Cook finally brought her clear. On January 17, about eight weeks after first reaching Maui, Cook sent capable, crusty master Bligh ashore to investigate an anchorage. Bligh returned and reported that he had found a bay that afforded a good anchorage and fresh water. Cook lost no time; by 11 A.M. he had brought the *Resolution* to anchor in what is now called Kealakekua Bay.

The ships' encircling cruise had caused great excitement throughout the island chain. Cook had been treated as a god a year earlier on the island of Kauai, but he was little prepared for the reception that he received at Hawaii. The delay in anchoring had given native priests time to concoct a theory about the visit. Cook was believed to be the departed god Lono, who had left the island ages ago, vowing to return in a great ship. Cook's arrival was a momentous occasion, to which inhabitants from all over the big island flocked out of curiosity and religious fervor.

Immediately after the ships anchored, the bay became alive with canoes. Cook was amazed: "I have no where in this sea seen such a number of people assembled at one place; besides those in the canoes all the shore of the bay was covered with people and hundreds were swimming about the ships like schools of fish." It was impossible to maintain order. The ships were crowded with laughing, curious Hawaiians (Cook called them "Indians," a term he used indiscriminately on Maori, Tahitians, Hawaiians, and Eskimo alike). The Englishmen were delighted to be treated so well. Cook remarked, "No women I ever met with were more ready to bestow their favors, indeed it appeared to me that they came with no other view."

One of the visitors was Koah, a priest who approached Cook with great veneration, draped him in a red cloth, and delivered a long chant.

He then presented the embarrassed Cook with a small pig and two coconuts. Shortly afterward Captain Cook, Lieutenant King, Koah, and a few others landed to look around the village. Innocently Cook found himself the principal of a highly ritualistic religious ceremony.

Cook's official journal ends with the January 17 entry.

Lieutenant King took over the journal after his captain was killed, and kept it faithfully until the *Resolution* returned to England. His account of the visit to Hawaii and the tragedy that followed is considered to be an accurate and fair version.

King's description of the ceremony was vivid. The party was led to a *morai*, a religious center, where a semicircle of idols focused on a quite putrid pig. Arranging the group around this grisly offering, Koah led Captain Cook up a rickety scaffold where he sat in discomfort and great risk of falling off. There followed a long continuation of chants and speeches with Cook in this awkward position. At length the exalted ones descended from the scaffold to a small square feasting area. A procession of natives carried in a baked pig and many side dishes. King and Cook were fed by their new friends, who tore off pieces of meat and put them into their mouths. However, King observed, Captain Cook, "recollecting the putrid hog, could not swallow a morsel, and his reluctance, as may be supposed, was not diminished, when the old man [Koah], according to his own mode of civility, had chewed it for him."

As soon as he could, Cook tactfully brought the proceedings to a conclusion, presenting a few presents to his hosts and returning to the ship. Hawaiian missionaries of the nineteenth century soundly criticized him for not denouncing the whole affair on the spot. It was, according to Christian belief, nothing else but blasphemy. However, the Englishmen could not understand the language, nor did they have any advance information about the Hawaiian god Lono. To them, this was just an elaborate, perhaps embarrassingly friendly reception. Although King recorded that the native ceremonies "approached adoration" of Captain Cook, none of his party realized that he was being worshiped as a god.

From that time on, Captain Cook suffered all the attentions due a deity. Whenever he went ashore, a priest accompanied him. Wherever he stopped, the place was made tabu.* He was always the center of a large procession whose approach was proclaimed to clear the way. Cook longed for the more simple treatment accorded him by his Tahitian and Tonganese friends. He liked to take walks, to explore coasts from his boat, and to question the natives about their habits and customs. The restrictions that accompanied adoration were galling. At first the priests would put the whole bay under tabu whenever Captain Cook disembarked from the *Resolution*. This brought a senseless halt to essential trade, because rank and file Hawaiians either obeyed the rules of tabu or were mercilessly punished. With much persuasion, Lieutenant King managed to get the harbor tabu lifted.

Cook sensed that these developments precluded a long carefree visit, like the ones he had enjoyed in the Society Islands. There he and his men were simply welcomed, and the length of their stay was not a problem. Trade flourished and good relations prevailed. But here in Hawaii, his requirements for food were raised by a levy on the populace and were presented as a gift to the god Lono. Under these conditions it would be easy to wear out a welcome. Cook resolved to complete necessary repairs and revictualing as quickly as possible, and leave Kealakekua Bay.

* A tabu place was one that had been designated as sacred; it would then be forbidden to walk upon it.

During the remainder of the month of January, ship's work progressed smoothly and relations with the natives were good. Everything came to a standstill, however, when King Terreeoboo returned from a visit to Maui and made a ceremonial canoe trip around the harbor. It was a magnificent sight. King Terreeoboo and his chiefs were dressed in "rich feathered coats and helmets, and were armed with long spears and daggers." Priests in the second canoe were surrounded by idols (probably *tikis*) which were covered with feathers. "Their eyes," King wrote of the idols, "were made of large pearl oysters, with a black nut fixed in the center; their mouths were set with a double row of the fangs of dogs, and, together with the rest of their features, were strangely distorted." The third canoe was filled with hogs and vegetables. This strange procession circled about the *Resolution* and then headed for shore. Captain Cook hastened there where Lieutenant King had drawn up a ceremonial guard of marines. They greeted King Terreeoboo with all the naval pomp and ceremony that they could muster, and retired to a tent for an exchange of gifts. Throughout this ceremony it was evident that Terreeoboo's friendship for Captain Cook was warm and genuine. In return for this greeting, in which he received a beautiful feather cloak and a canoe full of food, Cook presented Terreeoboo with a linen shirt and his sword.

Inevitably the visit of the *Resolution* and the *Discovery* put a strain on the islanders' resources. Soon the chiefs and priests began asking pointed questions about departure. Lieutenant King was very popular with the natives, so he questioned his friends to find out what the Hawaiians thought of Englishmen. "They imagined," he said, "we came from some country where provisions had failed, and that our visit to them was merely for the purpose of filling our bellies." They were also puzzled by "our having no women with us; together with our quiet conduct, and unwarlike appearance . . . We had now been sixteen days in the bay; and if our enormous consumption of hogs and vegetables be considered, it need not be wondered that they should wish to see us take our leave."

Cook informed Terreeoboo that they would leave in two days. Immediately a proclamation was issued throughout the village, and a final levy of food was gathered in. The Hawaiians openly rejoiced that the exciting visit was coming to an end. They overwhelmed the two ships with gifts of provisions and followed them well out to sea to say farewell. It was February 4, 1779.

Exactly a week later the ships came back. They had encountered a storm of such force that the *Resolution*'s foremast had given way. It could be repaired only at an anchorage, and Kealakekua was the only one that Cook had found. He realized that his return would not be popular, but he had no choice.

This time the welcome was subdued. The bay was quiet and its beaches were deserted. Inquiries revealed that Terreeoboo had departed and had left the bay in tabu. When he returned the next day, matters did not improve. The *Resolution*'s mast was landed ashore for repair, and astronomical instruments were set up in a tent near the morai. When it became clear that the return visit was to be one of some duration, the natives grew sullen. Thievery broke out, leading to irritation, loud arguments, and eventually to stone throwing at a watering party. In a misunderstanding the *Discovery*'s boat crew roughed up a friendly chief and narrowly escaped with their lives when angry natives attacked them with stones. When Captain Cook was informed of these incidents, he told King, "I am afraid that these people will oblige me to use some violent measures, for they must not be left to imagine that they have gained an advantage over us."

Lieutenant King spent a fitful night ashore in the tent, doubling his marine sentries as an added precaution. One sentry fired at a native marauder, who fled with several others, and afterward the night was strangely quiet. King went aboard the *Resolution* early the next morning (February 14) to find marines arming and Captain Cook loading his double-barreled gun. The *Discovery*'s cutter had been stolen during the night and Captain Cook planned to recover it with his usual method of holding important hostages. At the same time he gave orders to stop any canoes that attempted to leave the bay, and to seize them as additional persuasion to obtain the cutter's return. Both of these methods had worked on many past occasions, particularly with natives who knew the effect of firearms. This last order to seize canoes, however, backfired in Kealakekua Bay that fateful morning, and set off the spark that ignited mob violence.

Not anticipating serious resistance to his plans, Cook organized his expedition as follows: He sent Lieutenant King to one side of the bay to quiet the natives and to assure them that no harm would come to them. King was instructed to gather his own people together and be on guard. Four ship's boats, two each from the *Resolution* and the *Discovery*, were put on station in the bay to halt canoe traffic as mentioned earlier. Captain Cook planned to proceed to the opposite side of the bay with nine marines in the pinnace, accompanied by an armed party in the launch. Just before he left the ship, he gave orders to fire two "great guns" across the bay to head off some canoes.

Thus, on that ill-starred morning, the natives were aroused and fearful. They had heard rifles fired the night before, and they had just heard cannon fired from the ship. They knew of the various incidents that had caused irritation, so they expected some measures of retaliation. When Cook landed with his marine guard to look for King Terreeoboo, a great crowd began to gather.

The beach at this part of Kealakekua Bay was rocky, so Cook ordered his two accompanying boats to lie off-shore, close enough to render support if necessary. The officer in charge was Lieutenant Williamson, who had lost his self-control a year earlier during a beach incident at Kauai. Taking Lieutenant Phillips and his marine guard, Cook went to Terreeoboo's hut and asked the king and his two young sons to come on board the *Resolution* until the stolen cutter was returned. It was a friendly conversation and a reasonable request to which the king readily agreed. The two boys had been frequent guests aboard, so they ran delightedly down to the shore toward the boat. As Terreeoboo arose to leave, his favorite wife wept and begged him not to go. Others joined her, sensing that the king and his two sons were being taken as hostages. Two chiefs forcibly restrained the king, seizing his arms and making him sit down. The crowd pressed in so closely that the marine could not use their rifles. Lieutenant Phillips withdrew his men in a line toward the water's edge. The situation became tense.

Not wishing to shed blood, Captain Cook abandoned his plan, observing to Phillips that it would be impossible to compel Terreeoboo to accompany them without killing a great number of natives. Up to this point, Cook did not seem to be in any personal danger. However, a messenger dashed up to spread alarming news. One of the important local chiefs, Kalinau, had been killed when a patrol boat fired on his canoe. It was a senseless killing, which excited the crowd around Cook to a fever pitch. As he and Phillips began to walk slowly down to their boat, several natives made threatening gestures. One tried to stab Phillips, who knocked him down with the butt of his gun. Another threatened Cook with a stone and a dagger. The Captain fired one barrel of his gun—the one loaded with small shot— but the shot did not penetrate the man's matted armor. Thus encouraged, he and others pressed closer. Cook then fired the second barrel at the group, killing his closest tormentor. The marines also fired a volley into the crowd, but they did not have time to reload before the maddened mob overran them.

Contrary to Cook's expectations, the natives stood up under gunfire and did not panic. Phillips was stabbed in the shoulders, and he promptly shot his attacker before the blow could be repeated. The armed party offshore began firing into the crowd. Cook reached the water's edge, and was last seen calling to the boats to cease fire and come in. This was a fatal move. As long as he faced the crowd, no one would attack him, but when he turned to call the boat in, he was stabbed in the back. A great roar went up when Captain Cook fell into the water, and his body was dragged up on the beach, where it was "surrounded by the enemy, who snatching the dagger out of each other's hands, showed a savage eagerness to have a share in his destruction."

Phillips and five surviving marines scrambled to safety in the pinnace, which had pulled in toward shore. The other launch with its armed party, had, under the orders of Lieutenant Williamson, pulled the other way toward safety. It is generally conceded that prompt, effective action by Williamson might well have saved Captain Cook. At least the armed men could have rescued his body. But, as mentioned before, Lieutenant Williamson's timidness caused him to seek safety and the moment was lost.

The boats returned to their stunned ships. Lieutenant King's short journal entry describes the men's general feelings: "Thus fell our great and excellent Commander . . . How sincerely his loss was felt and lamented by those who had so long found their general security in his skill and conduct, and every consolation, under their hardships, in his tenderness and humanity, it is neither necessary nor possible for me to describe; much less shall I attempt to paint the horror with which we were struck, and the universal dejection and dismay which followed so dreadful and unexpected a calamity."

Cook's body was dismembered for a savage ritual purported by the Hawaiians to be reserved only for great chiefs. Whether his flesh was eaten is not known, but only some of his bones were finally returned several days later. Positive identification was made by a scar on his right hand. These remnants were buried at sea with great sorrow.

Clerke took command of the expedition until his

death from tuberculosis in August. Following Cook's humane example, he did not exact vengeance, but got the ships ready for sea. The burial was performed on February 21, and the ships left the next day. Here again they followed their leader's example by returning to the Arctic to continue his search for a northwest passage beyond Bering Strait. They were stopped once more by impenetrable ice, and finally turned back to Petropavlovsk for repairs. Leaving the Russian coast in October, 1779, with Lieutenant Gore in command, they returned to England a year later with a healthy crew. Cook's lessons had been well learned. The *Resolution* had lost five men by sickness, and the *Discovery* none, during the four-year voyage.

PART V

Genius Afloat

CHAPTER EIGHTEEN

PERSONAL LIFE AND CHARACTER

THERE is a wealth of information describing Captain Cook the great explorer, circumnavigator, and scientist. But there is very little that pictures him as a husband and father. It is presumed that his wife destroyed his personal letters. Three of Cook's six children died in their infancy. The two sons who followed their father into the navy met early deaths by drowning, and the third, who was destined for the church, died of fever while a student at Cambridge. Elizabeth Cook was left with her husband's medals and swords and an annual pension of £200. The proceeds of the Captain's published *Voyages*, as well as the small pension, were handled faithfully by her cousin, Isaac Smith, who looked out for her until his death in 1831. Smith had sailed with Cook on the *Endeavor* and had become a successful naval officer, retiring as a rear admiral. He left provisions for Mrs. Cook to be cared for by trusted servants after his death. When she died in 1835 she had outlived all of her close relatives and all of her husband's friends, and had drawn her pension for fifty-five years.

Self-educated, self-made Cook was an interesting man of many sides. The eulogies of his compatriots paint him as being self-controlled and almost saintly. Yet the missionaries of Hawaii damned him as immoral and blasphemous. Responsible study has proven the missionaries wrong, and the tributes of his friends more or less correct. The record shows that he was a dedicated, hardworking, courageous leader, who had an instinct for command, a love of the sea, and great trust in his fellowman. Justly famous in his own lifetime, he remained modest and unpretentious.

In closing a book of Cook's life and achievements, it is perhaps best to turn to the men who knew him and sailed with him. These friendly critics had entrusted their lives to his capable hands.

First, there was Lieutenant King, who wrote: "The qualities of his mind were of the same hardy, vigorous kind with those of his body. His understanding was strong and perspicacious; his judgment, in whatever related to the services he was engaged in, quick and sure. His designs were bold and manly, and both in conception, and in the mode of execution, bore evident marks of original genius. His carriage was cool and determined, and accompanied with an admirable presence of mind in the moment of danger. His manners were plain and unaffected. His temper might perhaps have been justly blamed as subject to hastiness and passion, had not these been disarmed by a disposition the most benevolent and humane.

"Such were the outlines of Captain Coo but its most distinguishing feature was t ting perseverance in the pursuit of his objec not only superior in the opposition of dangers, ..

pressure of hardships, but even exempt from the want of ordinary relaxation. During the long and tedious voyages in which he was engaged, his eagerness and activity were never in the least abated . . . to have conducted three expeditions of so much danger and difficulty, of so unusual a length, and in such a variety of situation with uniform and invariable success, must have required not only a thorough and accurate knowledge of his business, but a powerful and comprehensive genius. . . ."

Surgeon Stamwell sailed with Captain Cook on the third voyage, and consequently saw him as a mature leader and a veteran of ten years of discovery. His impression was: "Nature had endowed him with a mind vigorous and comprehensive, which in his riper years he had cultivated with care and industry. His general knowledge was extensive and various; in that of his profession he was unequaled. With a clear judgment, strong masculine sense, and the most determined resolution; with a genius particularly tuned for enterprise, he pursued his object with unshaken perseverance:—vigilant and active in an eminent degree: cool and intrepid among dangers: patient and firm under difficulties and distress: fertile in expedients: great and original in all his designs, active and resolved in carrying them into execution. These qualities rendered him the animating spirit of the expedition; in every situation he stood unrivaled and alone: on him all eyes were turned: he was our leading star. . . . He was beloved by his people, who looked upon him as a father, and obeyed his orders with alacrity."

These two tributes can be summed up very briefly as follows: Cook's intellect was great, but his character was greater. About such a man in the isolation of a lonely ship command, legend invariably grew. He was a heroic figure to the men of his ships as well as to the islanders of the South Pacific.

It is said that King George wept when he learned of Cook's death. So did Cook's men when they buried their captain in the waters of Kealakekua Bay. These tears would have been memorial enough for the austere, capable, and unpretentious James Cook.

CHAPTER NINETEEN

COOK'S LEGACY

JAMES COOK was more than an expert seaman and navigator. He was a true genius in the field of sea exploration. With a confidence born of years of experience and meticulous preparation, he sailed unknown seas well beyond the accepted limits of endurance. The results of his explorations were enhanced by his inquisitive mind and his passion for accuracy. He was original in method, intuitive in reasoning, and tireless in pursuing his goals. As an explorer, Captain Cook rose above mere competence and skill to a level of creative achievement that only a very few attained.

Fortunately, Cook lived in England at a time when exploration was important, and when scientific advances in navigation, cartography, and nautical medicine paved the way for his success. It was also the time of scientific revolution, when an organization devoted to science could wield a great influence on King George and the Royal Navy. If it had not been for the Royal Society's interest in the transit of Venus in 1769, James Cook would probably have gone down in history as a competent mapmaker and sometimes mathematician, who was "very expert in his business." Instead, the man and the times joined to produce discoveries and knowledge of immense importance. In his lifetime, his stature was such that the king of France and Spain wrote that "his discoveries benefit all nations." Benjamin Franklin called Cook "a friend of the human race." Explorers who followed him called him "the first of navigators." In all of these regards, his record speaks for itself.

Captain Cook has been called "a middle-brow genius" and "a genius of the matter-of-fact." These are good descriptions, because he was a practical man. For example, he knew that an ocean the size of the Pacific could be explored only by a ship that could stay at sea for long periods. Consequently he chose a squat, big-bellied collier from the merchant trade, instead of a faster, better armed ship. For his purposes the collier was more suitable. It could stand beaching for repair, but of more importance, it had ample space to carry a large supply of provisions. He crammed his ships with almost twice the "standard" navy ratio of food and supplies per man.

In all of his voyages he hoarded staple provisions like a miser, and fed his men fresh food whenever possible. He was the most faithful shopper the sea has known, going well out of his way to stop at isolated islands or ports for fresh water, fresh meat, and vegetables. To him these places were "vitamin stations" whose produce kept his crews healthy.

Cook was aware of the hazard of scurvy, having seen Captain Hugh Palliser of HMS *Eagle* bury twenty-two men and send one hundred and thirty to the hospital— all victims of scurvy contracted in a local cruise in the North Sea. It has been estimated that in the first twenty years of the seventeenth century, more than ten thousand European sailors died of the dread disease.

Scientists who studied the problem noted that scurvy sometimes occurred in cities or garrisons ashore. In these instances a cure was readily available, and miraculous recoveries resulted when scurvy patients were given fresh meat, green vegetables, and fruit. Aboard a sailing ship, particularly one that was becalmed at sea, the monotonous diet of salt beef and biscuits for week after week inevitably resulted in scurvy. The British Admiralty had promoted diet research many years before Cook began his first voyage. By 1768 the values of certain antiscorbutics were known, but it took a man of Cook's strength and determination to use them properly. The combination of antiscorbutics and his own innovations produced the secret of long voyages which made exploration of the Pacific possible. Cook believed that he would be remembered for his conquest of sea diseases long after his explorations were forgotten.

In that regard, it was his own dedication to accuracy that made him overemphasize the negative aspects of his voyages. Perhaps, too, this negative attitude stemmed from his many years before the mast as a noncommissioned officer. He was accustomed to obeying orders. To him the Admiralty's instructions read, "Go to the Pacific and find the unknown continent," or "Go to the Arctic and find a northwest passage." The fact that he proved that neither of these existed was immaterial to him. In his subconscious mind he believed that he had failed, and that he had let his superiors down. He did not realize just how much he was admired and cherished for his accomplishments. The lords of the Admiralty—seamen all—recognized bravery and understood hardship. They knew that not one officer in a thousand could duplicate Cook's thorough, systematic search of unknown waters. They, above all, appreciated the negative results and the consequent destruction of geographical theories. When the armchair geographers of London were routed by the cold facts of the voyages of the *Endeavor* and the *Resolution*, the Admiralty was greatly pleased and relieved. Great Britain was at war in 1775, and there were many other projects that demanded their lordships' attention.

In his geographical "failures," Captain Cook made significant contributions to knowledge and added a wealth of detailed data. As a matter of fact, he overwhelmed the British Admiralty with his observations. The documentation was complete and factual, and his claims were moderate. His journals had an air of scientific evaluation and the restraint of an intellectual skeptic.

None of his predecessors had made voyages of such length or had remained at sea for such long periods. Nor had any other explorers brought back such accurate observations. In his three voyages he established more order in the science of geography than the sum of all explorations in the preceding two hundred years. He circumnavigated the globe in high southern latitudes. In doing so, although he did not discover the continent of Antarctica, he set absolute limits to its sea boundaries. He cruised the pack ice of the Arctic, proving by his failure to penetrate it the impracticability of a merchant sea route. In spite of his opinion of the value of his work, the negative results of his explorations were of long-lasting importance.

Cook's geographical discoveries and his ability to fix them accurately rank him among the foremost world explorers. Captain La Perouse pointed out that the most ignorant man could be lucky and discover, but only the great had the capability to explore. Whenever Cook explored, he left a small monument to history. He insisted on precision, and would doggedly keep cruising off an unknown coast through weeks of stormy weather in order to finish a survey to his own satisfaction. During his third voyage, when he relied so much on the chronometer, he checked it repeatedly for accuracy. At Nootka Sound, where he stopped for four weeks, he used one hundred and thirty-seven lunar observations in a chronometer check.

Cook explored the Pacific from east to west, from the Antarctic to the Arctic. He completed the outline map of that great ocean by his exploration of the eastern coast of Australia and the western shorelines of Canada and Alaska. He filled in many of the blank spaces between, outlining New Zealand and the New Hebrides, and discovering new islands such as Hawaii and New Caledonia. Other bodies of land were rediscovered and fixed accurately.

The discoveries of British explorers in the Pacific resulted in English occupation of Australia, New Zealand, and several smaller island groups. The loss of Tahiti and New Caledonia to France, and the Hawaiian Islands to the United States, was one of default. During the age of discovery there were two popular doctrines of exploration in effect among the community of nations. Spain supported the doctrine of "prescriptive right," which permitted a country to earmark a discovery without actually using the unoccupied territory. England preferred the doctrine of "effective occupation," by which right of possesion went to the power that first occupied new land with a permanent garrison or settlement.

Under the leadership of William Pitt the Younger, England was willing to go to war in support of this doctrine. In the long run it may have been the wrong choice. Her later reluctance to garrison many British discoveries eventually saw them fall into other hands.

Solid geographical achievements and victory over disease were Cook's major contributions to humanity, but there were more. In the related fields of navigation, cartography, and seamanship, he had few, if any, equals. He was a supreme craftsman with the octant and chronometer and the best celestial navigator of his time. He had an instinct for the sea and made a lifetime study of its currents, winds, depths, and weather. His knowledge of sea environment and his ability to interpret signs saved him from shipwreck many times. British hydrographer Admiral Wharton admired Cook's extraordinary ability to chart unknown coasts, remarking that it "enabled him to originate, as it may be truly said he did, the art of modern marine surveying."

In the field of seamanship Cook had many competitors. It would be difficult to prove that he was supreme in this ancient skill, but the record shows that he was a master sailor. He knew ships, small boats, sails, rigging, and the use of ground tackle. He never lost a ship or one of his boats in the years that he spent coasting dangerous shores and landing through the surf. When he discovered Norfolk Island he made an immediate "routine" landing on the beach. A few years later when a colonizing party arrived off the island, the ship captain spent a frustrating week trying to get a boat ashore.

Cook's ability to sense danger has been mentioned, but it is best documented in the journal of a German sailor, Heinrich Zimmerman, who sailed on the third voyage. He said, "I had often noticed how confidently Cook faced the dangers of the ocean, and how well he knew them. But apart from this knowledge, he had also a remarkable flair for being able to foresee dangers before they actually happened. I was astonished to perceive that even here, off the shores of America in the midst of constant danger from rocks, shallows and sandbanks, Cook managed to pass his nights in undisturbed sleep. Yet it sometimes happened that he would come storming up on deck in the middle of the night and suddenly order a change of course. It often struck us that he must have received some sign or else had become clairvoyant.

"Now on the 24th of June—I remember the date exactly—we were sailing along the coast on a very foggy night. Nothing made us suspect any danger lurking in the darkness. Lieutenant Gore, whose watch it was, observed a sudden strong current, and would have sailed on happily, had not Cook suddenly rushed out of his cabin and in great agitation given the order to drop anchor at once . . . we were all amazed. The sailors stumbled on deck from all parts of the ship, asking what had happened, but no one could answer them for the ships were blanketed round by thick fog. Towards noon the following day the fog lifted sufficiently to let us see a rock rising steeply out of the sea, barely twenty paces ahead, and that the waters all round us were studded with rocks. There was no doubt but that neither of the ships would have been saved, had not Cook ordered the anchors to be dropped."

Cook trained a magnificent group of officers who carried out his theories of diet and practiced his inspired seamanship. Unfortunately many of them died while quite young, generally from the hardships and exposure of the long voyages, and were unable to go on to greater heights on their own. Three exceptions were Burney, Bligh, and Vancouver, whose accomplishments have already been described.

A farmer by birth and early training, Cook never lost his love for the land. With a farmer's instinct he was the "Johnny Appleseed of the Pacific." He introduced varieties of domestic animals to the various islands, scattering sheep, hogs, goats, cows, chickens, and dogs where there were none. He also gave away vegetable seeds, planted gardens, and introduced new strains of potatoes. He forecast the value of fur trade in North America; furs later became the great medium of exchange for the tea of China. As living evidence of his interest in animals there survives today (1966) in Tonga one of two turtles which Captain Cook presented to the island chief. The female has been dead for some time but the male is still alive and active despite his blindness.

Cook's observations of the life, crops, artifacts, languages, and traditions of the Pacific natives were treasure troves of information for anthropologists. He found that within a great sea triangle, bounded by Hawaii, New Zealand, and Easter Island, the Polynesian race had spread across the Pacific. They spoke variations of the same language, observed the same traditions, and worshiped the same gods. There was a great similarity in their canoes and crop produce. He noted that they did not have metal tools, knew nothing about the wheel, nor made any pottery. At the same time they showed advanced knowledge of the sea and had developed an ingenious primitive method of ocean navigation. He noted great differences between the Polynesians and the inhabitants of the New Hebrides and New Caledonia, who were Negroid, spoke a different language, and knew nothing about navigation. The Indians of North America, on the other hand, knew about the value and use of metals. The Eskimo, Cook noted, were well advanced in the art of living, considering the hardships of their climate. These observations from his journals are just a few of the important facts about the peoples of the Pacific that he recorded. Actually he wrote over one million words during his eleven years of discovery, and a great portion of his literary work dealt with the people he met.

Cook's attitude toward the natives of all places was one of paternal benevolence. He insisted on gentle treatment and honesty, and recognized the foibles of his savage friends. He consistently punished his own men for crimes committed against the natives, and while it was impossible to protect the islanders from the spread of venereal disease, he tried manfully to do this. Cook's humanitarian policies were remembered in the Pacific long after he died.

Perhaps it is fitting to conclude this account of his life with a little-known testimonial which originated on the bleak coast of Siberia. Shortly after the third voyage was over, the governor of Kamchatka reported to St. Petersburg that he had achieved an unusual diplomatic triumph. The Tchuktches, a stubborn, warlike tribe that inhabited the eastern coast of Siberia, had long resisted Russian approaches. They now announced that they were ready to sign a treaty of peace and friendship. They gave as their reason the courteous and friendly treatment that they had received when visited by two ships manned by white men. The governor was honest. He admitted to the home government (but not to the Tchuktches) that the two ships had been the *Resolution* and the *Discovery*, under the command of Captain James Cook.

REFERENCES

BEAGLEHOLE, J. C. *The Exploration of the Pacific*. London: Macmillan, 1934.

BEAGLEHOLE, J. C. (ed.) *The Journals of Captain James Cook*. Cambridge: Cambridge University Press, Vol. I 1955, Vol. II 1961.

CARRINGTON, A. H. *Life of Captain Cook*. London: Sidgewick & Jackson Ltd., 1939.

GOULD, LIEUTENANT COMMANDER R. T. *Captain Cook*. London: Gerald Duckworth Co., 1935.

GWYTHER, JOHN M. *Captain Cook and the South Pacific*. Boston: Houghton, 1955.

KITSON, ARTHUR. *Captain James Cook*. London: 1907.

MUIR, REAR ADMIRAL JOHN R. *Life and Achievements of Captain James Cook*. Toronto: Ryerson Press, 1939.

PRICE, A. GRENFELL. *The Exploration of Captain James Cook*. New York: Heritage Press, 1958.

VANDERCOOK, JOHN W. *Great Sailor*. New York: Dial Press, 1951.

WHARTON, CAPTAIN W. J. L. *Captain Cook's Journal*. London: E. Stock, 1893.

WILLIAMSON, JAMES A. *Cook and the Opening of the Pacific*. New York: Macmillan, 1948.

CHRONOLOGY OF CAPTAIN COOK
Early Life 1728–1768

Oct., 1728	Born in village of Marton in Yorkshire, England
1747	Goes to sea as apprentice
1752	Becomes mate of collier *Friendship*
1755	Enlists as seaman in Royal Navy
1756	Appointed boatswain of *HMS Eagle*
1757	Appointed warrant master of *HMS Pembroke*
1758–62	Surveys and charts St. Lawrence River and coasts of Canada
1762	Marries Elizabeth Batts in London
1762–66	Surveys coasts of Newfoundland
1766	Observes eclipse off Newfoundland
1768	Appointed lieutenant in Royal Navy; takes command of *Endeavor*

First Voyage

July, 1768	Sails from Plymouth on 26th for Rio de Janeiro, via Madeira
Dec.	Departs Rio de Janeiro on 8th

Jan., 1769	Doubles Cape Horn
April	Lands at Tahiti
Oct., 1769–Mar., 1770	Explores coasts of New Zealand
Apr., 1770	Lands at Australia
Sept.	Lands at Batavia
Mar., 1771	Reaches Cape Town
July	Returns to England

Second Voyage

July, 1772	Sails from Plymouth for Cape Town
Oct.	Returns to Cape Town
Dec., 1772–Mar., 1773	Cruises Antarctic; returns to New Zealand, March 26
July–Nov.	Cruises Society and Friendly Islands
Dec., 1773–Feb., 1774	Makes second Antarctic cruise
Mar.–Oct., 1774	Lands at Easter Island; returns to Tahiti and Friendly Islands
Nov.–Dec.	Cruises ice edge to Cape Horn
Jan.–Mar., 1775	Cruises ice edge to Cape Town
July	Returns to England

Third Voyage

July, 1776	Sails for Cape Town
Nov., 1776–Feb., 1777	Cruises Antarctic to New Zealand
Mar.–Aug., 1777	Cruises tropic islands; visits Tahiti
Jan., 1778	Discovers Hawaii

Feb.–Mar., 1778	Sails from Hawaii to coast of Oregon
Mar.–Oct.	Cruises coasts of Alaska and Siberia
Nov., 1778–Jan., 1779	Returns to Hawaii
Feb., 1779	Captain Cook killed in Hawaii on Feb. 14
Feb., 1779–Oct., 1780	Cook's ships make another Arctic cruise and return to England

INDEX

A

Aborigines of Australia, 67, 71

Adventure (ship), 57, 87, 89, 95, 98, 105, 108
  massacre, 107, 138

Agincourt (ship), 137

Alaska, 145, 151, 175
  Gulf of, 148

Alaska Peninsula, 148, 149

Aleutian Islands, 144, 148, 149, 151

America, 16

American colonies, 134

American Revolution, 3

Amsterdam Island. *See* Friendly Islands

Annamocka (Rotterdam), 120

Anson, George, 4, 18

Antarctic, 18, 34, 93
  Cook's exploration of, 94–96, 108–113, 122
  weather in, 96, 105, 109, 113

Antarctic Circle, 94, 109–110

Antarctic convergence, 95

Antarctica, 174

Arctic, 163, 174

Arctic Circle, 150

Arnold, John, 90

Ascension Isle, 128

Atlantic Ocean, 9, 11, 12, 19, 126, 134

Australia, 17, 18, 65, 66, 74, 97
  Cook's visit to, 67–73, 175

Australia del Espiritu Santo, 113, 120, 122

B

Baffin Bay, 134, 149

Balboa, Vasco Nuñez de, 15

Baltic, 5, 6

Banks, Joseph, 23–24, 36, 37, 41, 45, 50, 52, 60, 67, 70–71, 75, 81, 87, 90
  on Cook's behavior during disaster, 68
  on death of John Radon, 53
  on leaving inhospitable Rio de Janeiro, 38
  relations with Tahitian natives, 46, 51
  relationship with Cook, 24, 87

Banks Peninsula, 55, 61

Batavia, 18, 65, 72, 74
  malaria in, 75–78

Bay of Biscay, 31

Bay of Success, 39, 41

Bayley, Astronomer, 90, 103, 136

Bering Strait, 145, 150, 163

Bering, Vitus, 144–145, 151

Bligh, William, 136, 149, 153, 178

Botany Bay, 67